Cover: Dallin. *Indian Archer*. c. 1914. Giust Gallery.

CYRUS E. DALLIN:

HIS SMALL BRONZES AND PLASTERS

Kent Ahrens

Introductory Essay

Fred Licht

ROCKWELL MUSEUM

Corning, New York, 1995

Exhibition Dates: April 16–August 27, 1995

111 Cedar Street
Corning, New York 14830

Library of Congress Catalogue Card Number: 94-62134
ISBN: 0-9622038-6-6

Distributed by the University of Washington Press
P.O. Box 50096
Seattle, Washington 98101-2604

Funding for the exhibition and publication has been made available
in part by generous gifts from:

Arnot Realty Corporation
The Chase Manhattan Corporation
Chemung Canal Trust Company
Dresser-Rand Company
Mrs. Amory Houghton
The Woodcock Foundation

ACKNOWLEDGMENTS

I wish to express my most sincere thanks to Fred Licht for responding favorably to my request that he share his thoughts on monumental sculpture in America.

Rell G. Francis, author of *Cyrus E. Dallin. Let Justice Be Done*, has been a source of information and support during the course of my research for the exhibition.

Royal W. Leith, Catherine A. Chelak and Robert Schweitzer patiently reread my manuscript and made valuable suggestions for its improvement, while at the same time offering me encouragement for the project.

Many individuals have my gratitude for their information and assistance in many ways: Bob and Hertha Rockwell, Ruth Dallin Stevenson, Morton C. Bradley, Vern G. Swanson, Robert O. Davis, Thomas C. Proctor, Susana Forster-Castillo, Jonathan L. Fairbanks, Robert Shure, Lino Giust, Laura S. Griffith, Annette Blaugrund, Barbara J. MacAdam, Judy L. Larson, Kathryn Talalay, Daniel C. Swan, Rick Stewart, Kathryn Greenthal, Gail F. Serfaty, Alain Joyaux, George Gurney, Kathleen O'Malley, Marie Pulsone Woods, Patricia C. Fitzmaurice, Anne Morand, Frances Petty Sargent, Selma Koss Holtz, Betsy Johnson, Deborah J. Ervin, George Horse Capture, Joseph W. Smith, Joy S. Collins, Katherine W. Burg, Robert P. Metzger, Paula Stewart, Brian W. Dippie, Nanepashemet, Russell H. Gardner, James P. McGough, Marjorie D. Conder, Rhonda L. Butler, Mark Brown, Christine Hennessey and Reno Pisano.

The staffs of numerous libraries and archives across the country helped make my research both pleasant and profitable, and at the risk of omitting one or another, thanks are due: The Corning Museum of Glass; Archives of American Art; The Church of Jesus Christ of Latter-day Saints, Historical Department—Archives; The Arlington Historical Society; Hanover Area Historical Society; Onondaga Historical Association; Missouri Historical Society Library; Woolaroc Museum; Kansas City Public Library; Gilcrease Museum; Buffalo Bill Historical Society; Amon Carter Museum; Mary Institute and Saint Louis Country Day School; Amon Carter Museum; Dartmouth College; Brown University; Central High School, Tulsa; Pilgrim Hall Museum; Longyear Museum and Historical Society; Museum of Fine Arts, Boston; Springville Museum of Art; Fairmount Park Art Association; Historical Society of Pennsylvania; Drexel University; Massachusetts College of Art; Pioneer Woman Museum; University of Virginia; Library of Congress.

Finally, I wish to thank the entire staff of the Rockwell Museum for their support. Mercedes Skidmore in particular deserves a note of recognition for her unfailing assistance, Andrew M. Fortune helped greatly with the photography, and Susan E. Kowalczyk coordinated the loans.

Kent Ahrens
Director

LENDERS

American Academy of Arts and Letters

Amon Carter Museum

Anonymous Lender

Ball State University Museum of Art

Diplomatic Reception Rooms, Department of State

Richard L. Fisher

Gilcrease Museum

Giust Gallery

Michael D. Greenbaum

Heckscher Museum

Sandra Rockwell Herron

High Museum of Art

Hood Museum of Art, Dartmouth College

Longyear Museum and Historical Society

Mongerson-Wunderlich Galleries

Museum of Church History and Art

Museum of Fine Arts, Boston

National Museum of American Art

The New-York Historical Society

Rockwell Museum

Springville Museum of Art

Ruth Dallin Stevenson

Textron Inc.

Town of Arlington, Massachusetts

University of Virginia Library

RANDOM THOUGHTS OF AN OUTSIDER: MONUMENTAL SCULPTURE IN AMERICA

Fred Licht

Since I have never been an Americanist, I paid only peripheral and scant attention to American monumental sculpture until I learned that there existed a monument to the boll weevil somewhere in Alabama (Fig. 1). I was told about it as a joke, and at first I registered it as such until it occurred to me that the conception of a monument to a negative power represented something unique and significant in the history of Western celebratory sculpture. Since then I have had more than one occasion to think about America's contribution to the field of monumental sculpture and though I have never studied the subject in any disciplined manner, I was delighted when Kent Ahrens granted me an opportunity of "going public" with the speculations and ideas I had hitherto kept strictly to myself. What follows is therefore by no means a reliable text on the history of American monumental sculpture but simply the ruminations of someone who has stumbled inadvertently on a fascinating and puzzling phenomenon.

The birth of the American nation coincides with the appearance of the first symptoms that foretell of the death of a five-thousand-year-old tradition of monumental sculpture. If it took America nearly a century to come to terms with the conflict between the desire of public, permanent expression of the nation's ideals, and the conditions of a modern age which was hostile to just such a form of expression, the fault lay not entirely with the cultural uncertainties of the young nation but with conditions that demanded the redefinition of what was meant by monumental sculpture all over the Western world. Over and above these universal problems besetting the category of monumental sculpture, there appeared other aspects of the universal malaise that are peculiar to the gradually emerging culture that was specifically American in nature. In many ways the difficulties and contradictions that attend the slow emergence of an American monumental idiom ultimately bedeviled not only America but the rest of the world as well. Seen from this angle, America's unresolved hesitations vis-à-vis monumental sculpture ultimately made the United States the battleground for all the major decisions regarding public monuments. Let us turn first to the general, international problems surrounding monumental sculpture during the fateful last quarter of the 18th century that saw the birth both of the United States and of the modern epoch in which we still live. Obviously, only a simple listing of those forces which militate against the tradition of public monumental sculpture can be undertaken within the framework of this introduction.

1. Beginning with the decades of the American and French revolutions, the Western world entered into a revolutionary epoch. Naturally, there had been precedents for both the American and French revolutions, most

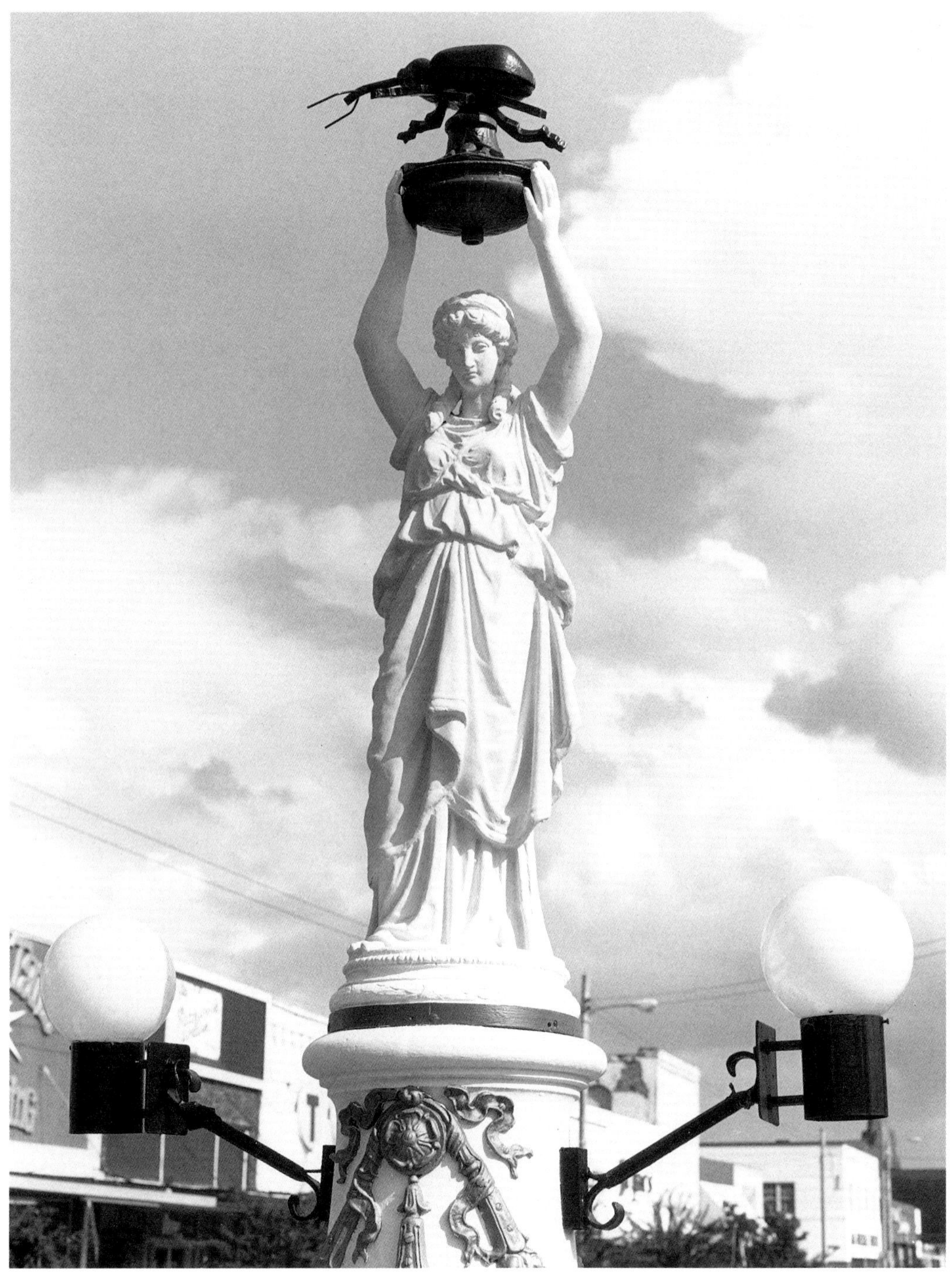

Fig. 1. *Boll Weevil Monument*. 1919/1949-54. Cast iron, lead and aluminum. Enterprise, Alabama. The female figure (3 feet) was dedicated in 1919, with the boll weevil designed by Luther Baker in 1949, and a replacement cast made in 1954. Courtesy Dan Brothers, Staff Photographer, Alabama Bureau of Tourism and Travel.

notably, the English revolution of the 17th century. Yet these earlier revolutions did not change the essential tenor of Western civilization. Fundamental beliefs in a system of ethical, religious and political values remained unshaken. With the two major revolutions at the end of the 18th century, all beliefs, all traditions become subject to revision. In such a climate, monuments become more and more untenable, because it is the function of monuments to be "reactionary," i.e., to project the values of the past onto the future. In France, home of one of the most grandiose traditions of monumental sculpture, the great revolution that begins with the storming of the Bastille never contemplated the erection of monuments to transmit to future generations the momentous events that were changing every aspect of human existence. If monumental sculpture comes to a dramatic (if temporary) end in France, how much more problematic must the notion of such celebratory sculpture seem in the United States where there had never existed any form of monumental sculpture. From this moment on, monumental, celebratory sculpture, after being considered the noblest, most admirable form of expression in the visual arts, enters into a period in which it is regarded always with suspicion and usually with hostility.

2. Monuments depend on the commonly shared belief in eternity. Sculpture in general but monumental sculpture in particular would make no sense at all, given the expense and effort involved, if it didn't hold out the promise of enduring for all time. Almost all Western religions deal with time in both its profane and its sacred manifestation. Profane time stretches beyond the limits of the human imagination until such a time as God brings all temporality to an end to institute a universal judgment. It is at this point that the world as we know it disappears followed by timeless eternity.

Monuments, though they are often spoken about as "eternal," are always thought to live for the span of profane time. It is during this span that they fulfill their function of transmitting the ideals and beliefs of the past to a vast future. At the end of profane time, all monuments along with the totality of the physical world will disappear, since their function of making manifest Divine Will will have been fulfilled.

This duality of profane and sacred time is denied by the epoch ushered in by the American and French revolutions. This new attitude as related to monumental sculpture is most succinctly expressed in Shelley's *Ozymandias*. Here, for the first time, monuments are attacked for their vain futility.

For the 19th and 20th centuries it will be Shelley's concept of monumental sculpture that will prevail in the minds of cultural leaders. The one great quality of monumental sculpture which justified its very existence, endurance, is mocked.

3. Monumental sculpture is only viable if the communality for whose spiritual benefit a monument is erected recognizes and believes in a certain number of fixed values that express the will of God. Thus a great military victory is seen as more than just a historical fact but as a decision due to Divine intervention. Once this cohesive system of communal beliefs is shattered and is supplanted by purely private religious and ethical options, public monuments in which the communality sees embodied its highest ideals, become unwarrantable.

4. Concomitant with the religious aspects of sculpture are the changes in values that surround all events and individuals after the revo-

lutionary years at the end of the 18th century. To the artists and the public before our epoch, it was perfectly obvious that some kings, some generals, some popes had been better or worse than others, and that some kings, generals, or popes had been downright criminal in their actions. But this perception in no way undermined the sanctity of the office they represented. It was understood that more than the individual, it was the power behind that individual's destiny which was celebrated by the monument. And that power was without appeal. The king was king by the Grace of God. A ruler instituted by the will of the majority of the population has no such backing, nor can his deeds be said to represent Divine resolve.

5. As important as any of the impalpable considerations listed above is the more pragmatic question of economics. Unlike its sister art of architecture, sculpture is not necessity, and unlike its sister art of painting, sculpture (even when it is on a modest scale) is very costly indeed. Not only are the materials expensive but the sculptor needs rent for a studio large enough to judge colossal effects, and he needs assistants for the cutting of stone or the casting of metal.

The ruler of pre-revolutionary times was not answerable for expenses incurred in the erection of a monument. Nor was his choice of artist, of iconography or setting subject to anything but his will. A parliamentary representative will hesitate to spend public funds for what is bound to be considered a luxury by the majority of his constituents. Just as damaging to the commissioning of monumental sculpture in modern times is the question of patronage. Kings or popes had invariably enjoyed an education which put them on a par with the artists they employed. Their choice of artist depended more on their financial ability to secure the services of the best available sculptor than on their recognition of who was the greatest available artist. The same cannot be said, alas, for the majority of our parliamentarians whose educational baggage rarely includes thorough training in any of the arts. The choice of artist will therefore inevitably unleash public controversy in which they once again stand to lose a lot of votes.

If these major considerations...and many more of minor kind...weighed heavily on the survival of monumental sculpture in post-revolutionary Europe, American artists who aspired to create a native monumental tradition were faced with still more, specifically American inhibitions towards the realization of such a dream.

1. Monuments flourish in stable and cohesive communities. Unless one feels that one's children and their children will continue to live in the same place, one will think twice to erect commemorative monuments. American society is characterized by constant mobility motivated in part by the tempting prospect of vast empty regions waiting for settlers, in part by the intense individuality both of Americans and of the successive waves of immigrants who, having once had the strength to uproot their lives, find it easy to keep on moving. The "Go West, young man" attitude is not an invention of Horace Greely's. The Puritan settlements in Massachusetts were hardly a generation old when Roger Williams and his friends broke away to settle in Rhode Island.

Perhaps it is instructive to compare American and French attitudes in this respect, French society in spite of the mass migrations caused by the Industrial Revolution being the most homogeneous. There is hardly a town of respectable size in all of France that does not have its monument to Louis Pasteur. Now, without wanting to diminish Pasteur's importance, his discoveries (cures for anthrax, rabies, and vine mildew) touch the lives of an infinitesimal fraction of humanity. Dr. William Morton's discovery of anesthesia at Massachusetts General Hospital has benefited the majority of men and women the world over, generation after generation. There exists a modest monument to him (Fig. 2) hidden among the plantings of Boston's Public Garden (although hardly any Bostonians know of it), but the idea of raising a monument to Dr. Morton in Chicago or Pittsburgh or San Francisco strikes one as ridiculous. Proud as Americans are of their nation and their nationality, the concept of what constitutes either of these abstractions is extremely fugitive and based more on private experience than on public education forging a nation based on a common historical and cultural heritage.

2. The fact that neither the materials nor the techniques for manipulating them were readily available in America throughout most of the 19th century drove the ambitious young American sculptor abroad (Horatio Greenough, Hiram Powers, Hendrik Christian Anderson). For the most part, these sculptors found working conditions so much better in Italy that they often decided to stay. In Italy or in Europe generally, they could also anticipate a more understanding public response to their ambitions. With rich Americans making it a habit to travel extensively in Europe, American sculptors residing in Rome, Florence or Paris could count on staying in close touch with American developments and with the American market.

3. Monuments require an urban civilization (Fig. 3). In Europe, it was taken for granted that all civilization *was* urban. In America the balance between rural and urban wasn't tipped in favor of the latter until after the Civil War.

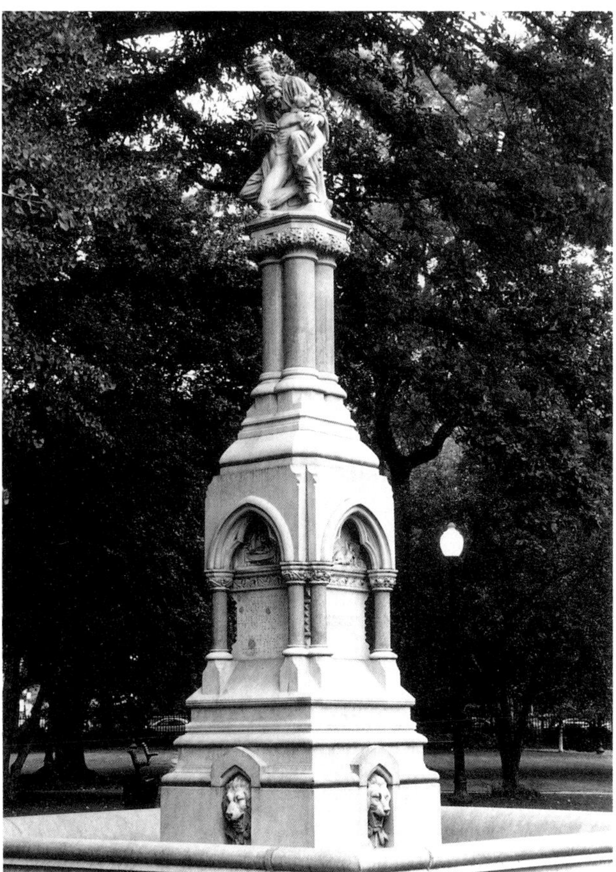

Fig. 2. John Quincy Adams Ward. *The Ether Monument.* 1868. Public Garden, Boston.

The predominance of a rural culture in America may have had a somewhat detrimental effect on the creation of a native tradition of monumental sculpture during the 19th century, but it suddenly and unexpectedly turned to being an advantage in our own time. The conceptions of Gutzon Borglum would probably have been inconceivable by any but an American mind.[1]

In our own century the idea (totally ludicrous to European minds) of monuments located in rustic isolation may very well have made "land art" a possibility in America (Fig. 4). The

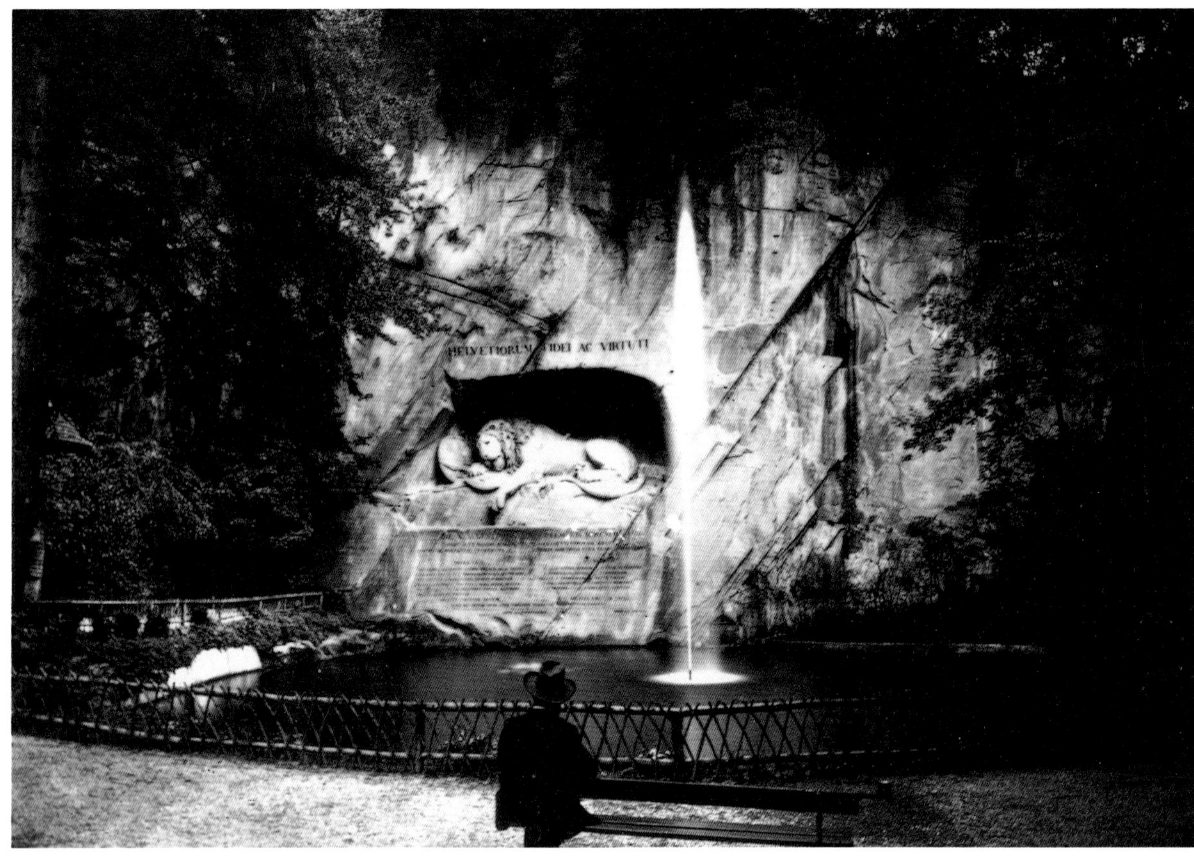

Fig. 3. Bertel Thorvaldsen. *The Lion of Lucerne.* 1819-21. Lucerne, Switzerland.
Photograph Courtesy of The Photographic Archives, National Gallery of Art.

idea of a monument existing unseen except by means of the nearly disembodied photographic reproduction is typical of the ease with which American sculpture turns the most revered and unquestioned tenets of sculpture upside down. It is just another example of the sort of thing most familiar in the work of Alexander Calder. For millennia it was taken for granted that all sculpture had to stand on the ground. Calder, without hesitation, cut the ground from under sculpture and redefined the whole nature of the art.

4. The most complicated problem faced by all American sculptors, especially by those interested in monumental dimensions and monumental values, has, to my knowledge, been touched on only peripherally by historians of American art. Yet it is a crucial question that is equally important when viewed from the point of view of the tradition of sculpture in the west or from the point of view of American civilization.

Monumental sculpture, in the final analysis, has always been deeply motivated and justified by religion. Even when monuments have a (seemingly) dynastic or political intent, the power relied on by dynasty or politics is always of a religious nature. Up to the moment of the Protestant Reformation, this condition worked in favor of the commissioning and the creation of public sculpture. During the first, most radical decades of the Reformation, the First

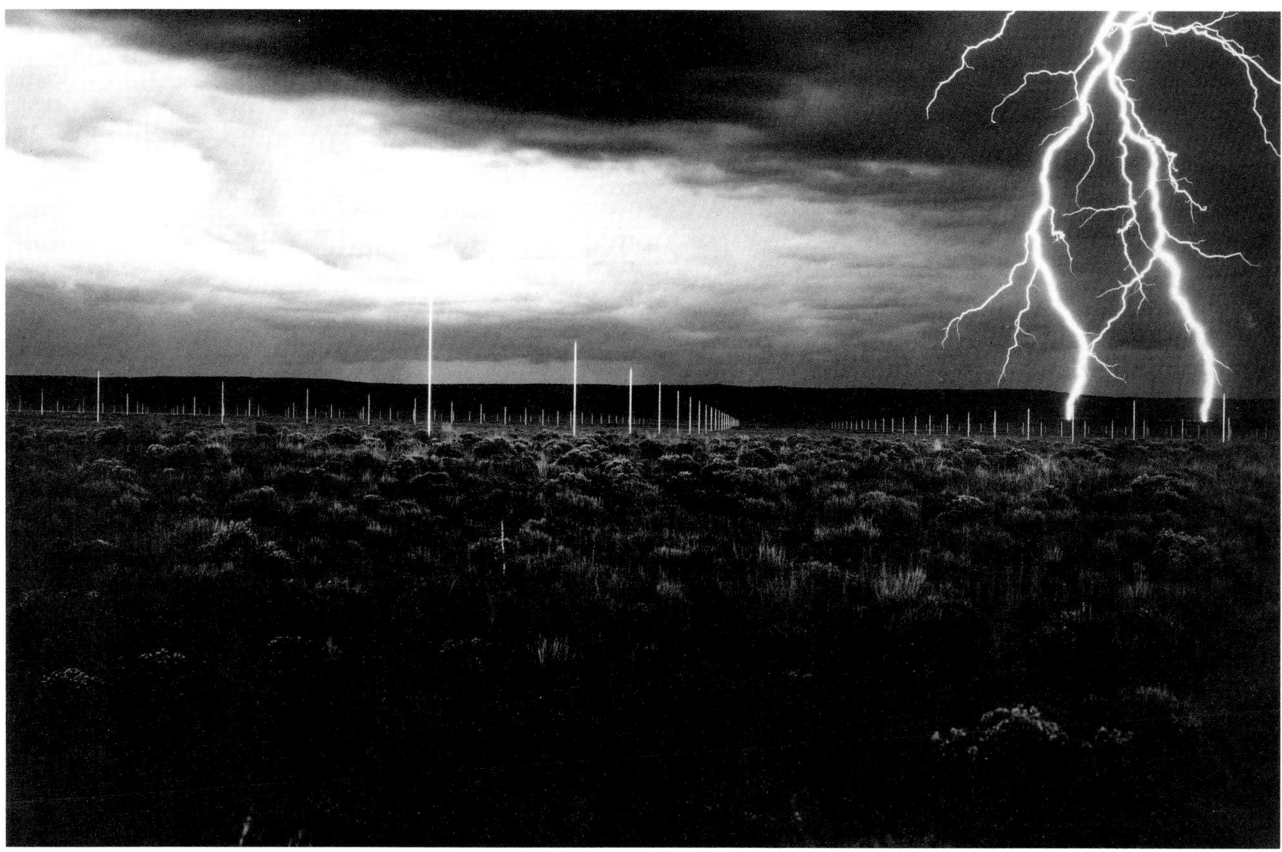

Fig. 4. Walter De Maria. *The Lightning Field*. 1977. Albuquerque, New Mexico. Courtesy DIA Center for the Arts. Photo Credit: John Cliett.

Commandment was invoked to unleash a violent iconoclasm to which immeasurable treasures fell victim. Indeed, the charge made by Protestants against Roman Catholicism that it was by nature idolatrous was so fraught with emotional intensity that it weighed heavily against Catholicism in the ensuing struggle for the allegiance of Christian souls caught in the struggle between Catholicism and Reform.

In the states which emerged as Protestant powers, the iconoclastic fervor of Protestantism's early years ebbed very quickly and was gradually reversed as the Protestant dynasties eagerly reached out for all those instruments of propaganda which had served their Catholic ancestors (and contemporaries) so well. For the most part, the Protestant states when they were still Catholic had been strong in the art of painting and less endowed with great sculptural talents. Now, as Protestant states, they were capable of engendering schools of painting (which appealed to their mercantile natures as paintings could easily be bought and sold) while sculpture was nearly non-existent for both economic as well as religious reasons (sculpture answering more closely to the definition of "graven image" than painting did).

To fill the growing demand for dynastic sculpture, therefore, most of the Protestant nations depended on importing foreign talents. This is especially true of the Scandinavian kingdoms, of England and of those German states that were not Catholic, yet needed sculpture as a dynastic appurtenance. All of these countries, of course, since they had originally been Catholic, could count on a high degree of appreciation of sculpture. Gradually this situation brought about a slow but steady production of native sculptors with Sweden and Denmark in the lead, until by the end of the 18th century such artists as Wiedewelt, Flaxman, Sergel and Trippel could actually compete with Canova and Houdon. With the death of Canova, leadership in the art of sculpture passed for long decades into the hands of the Protestant Dane, Thorvaldsen.[2]

If sculpture had suffered a near-fatal blow with the Reformation in the Protestant parts of Europe, its status in an America that had no Catholic memories whatsoever and was more Protestant in outlook than European Protestants, was bound to be far more precarious...a situation which still survives in most American museums where the departments responsible for the acquisition and display of sculpture are usually termed "Department of Sculpture and Decorative Arts," for it is only as weathervanes or other minor decorative objects that sculpture was originally tolerated at all by early America.

Proof of the unquenchable need mankind feels to commemorate certain events and great personalities is that the drive towards the creation of a monumental sculpture, which would express America's most cherished values, grew constantly throughout the 19th century in spite of what seemed overwhelming obstacles.

Even before a generation of American sculptors arose that could think in terms of marble or bronze, William Rush, who only knew how to deal with clay and wood, attempted something approaching monumental dignity in his *George Washington* (Fig. 5) in Philadelphia.[3] Only with Greenough do we begin to have "immortal longings" to work for the nation instead of working for collectors. There followed the work of such artists as Crawford, who though not yet ready for public monuments, clearly displayed both the desire and the ability to conceive of sculpture on the grand scale.[4]

Given the general attitude of rejection or downright hostility towards monumental sculpture, it is amazing to see that there is nevertheless an undercurrent in American civilization that ardently wishes to see America become preeminent in just this field. The *locus classicus* of such hope is, of course, Hawthorne's *Marble Faun* where American sculptors (of a certain kind) are extolled as bearing the banner of America's most admirable virtues and aspirations. Not long after, Henry James, never one to sound the super-patriotic note, predicts nevertheless in *Roderick Hudson* that the making of sublime monuments will be the crowning achievement of the United States. Such a statement must have seemed quixotic at the time but, in retrospect, one can see that there were already some symptoms on the American scene that indicated a change of heart. I refer to the enormous sculptural programs that were part and parcel of the great exhibitions organized in Philadelphia, Chicago, St. Louis and Buffalo. Though most of this statuary was of an impermanent kind, it did alert the widest possible public to the necessity and the dignity of public sculpture.[5] Naturally, the path from the sculpture of the great Expositions to the work done by our major sculptors today is long and difficult...too long and too difficult to be surveyed here. Yet it is evident now that Henry James's bold prophecy has been fulfilled. We need only cite the *Vietnam Memorial* (Fig. 6) in Washington to prove our point.

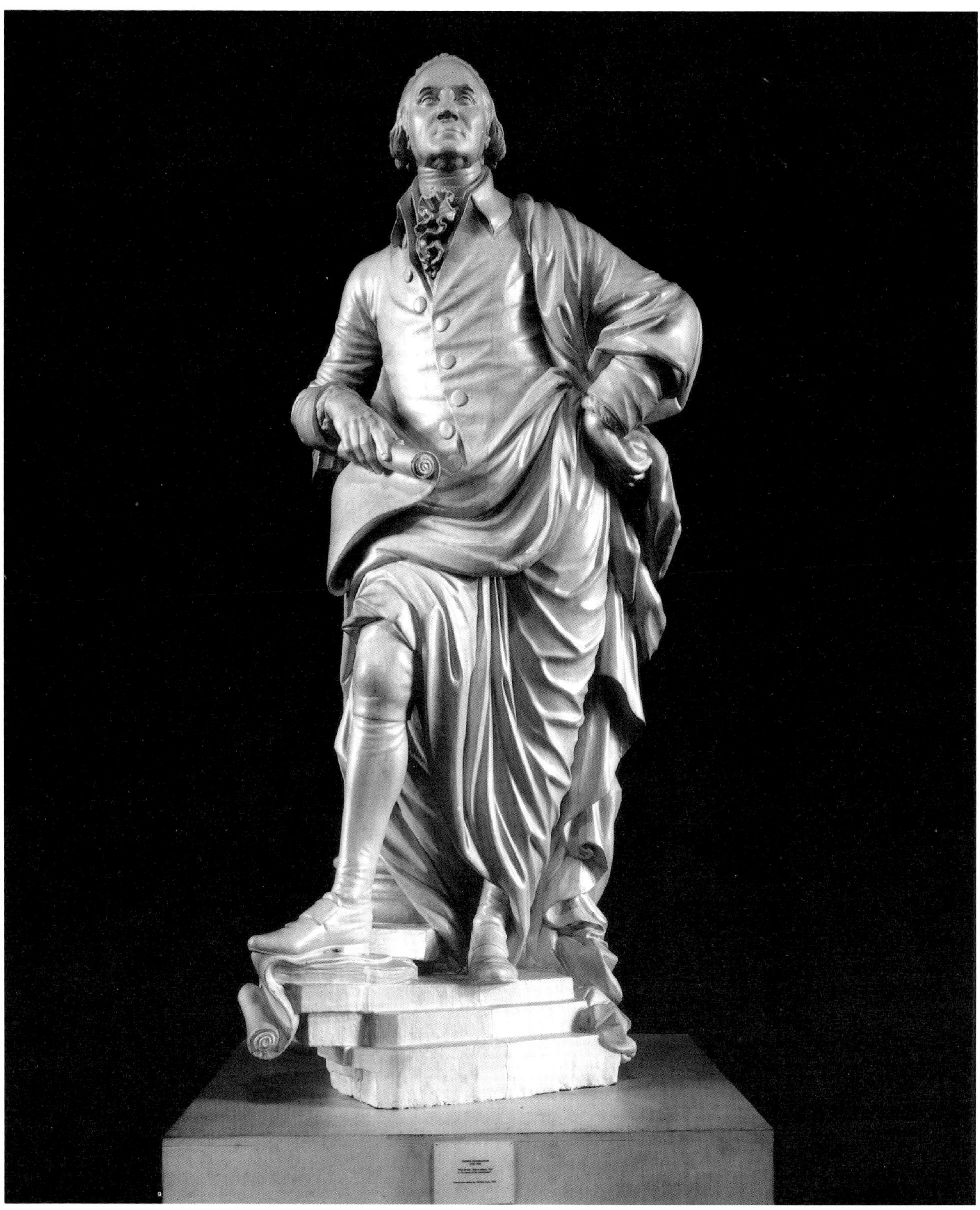

Fig. 5. William Rush. *George Washington*. 1814. Pine. Philadelphia. Courtesy Independence National Historical Park.

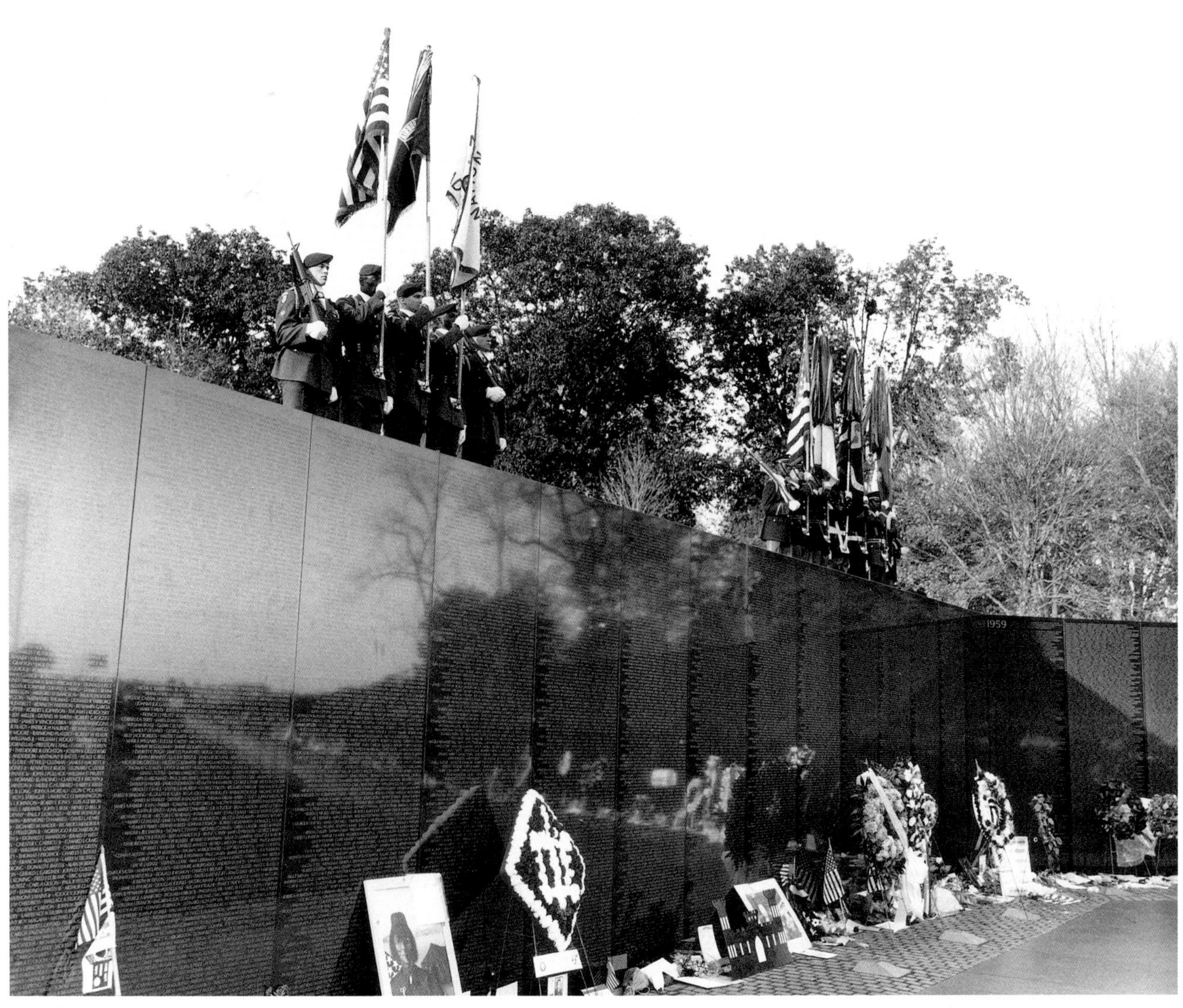

Fig. 6. Maya Ying Lin. *Vietnam Veterans Memorial.* 1982. Washington, D.C. Courtesy National Park Service.

Naturally, when one says "Vietnam Memorial" what one ought to mean is both the architectural and the figural monument which form an ideal unity expressive of the nature and the condition of American monuments. The war in Vietnam was not only a single-minded war fought by Americans against a distant enemy. It was also a war that pitched opposing American ideals against each other. The multiplicity of moral consciousness that marks American civilization has never been so completely and openly manifest. It was a tragic internecine conflict, but it was also symptomatic of America's remarkable ability to develop in a vast number of often diametrically opposed directions. And since public monuments always are (or should be) deeply bound up with communally held spiritual values, the esthetically and morally antagonistic components of the *Vietnam Memorial* in Washington are an indication of America's continuing flexibility and growth. No other nation has been able to express the ambiguous nature of modern warfare as thoroughly, as impressively, as honestly as America has. Nor, of course, is the *Vietnam Memorial* alone in representing America's enduring contribution to a mode of expression that has always represented one of mankind's highest achievements.

* * * * *

To go from William Rush's *George Washington* to the work of contemporary builders of American monuments, dealing only with the standard masterpieces of American monumental sculpture, is unjustifiable. As has been demonstrated, the road was unusually arduous and unusually fraught with traps, detours and obstacles unknown to other civilizations. The triumphs predicted by Hawthorne and James were won in a vast series of battles, some of which were victories, while others ended in defeat. Surveyed as a whole, the history of American monuments depends on the contribution of many artists whose work and lives have been obscured by time and negligence. During Cyrus Dallin's lifetime, men like James were quite alone in being able to appreciate the importance of public sculpture and deplore its lack on the American scene. It is against this panorama of misunderstanding, hostility and ignorance that the work of the early sculptors who began to convert American taste and American ideas must be measured. In this guise, the work of Dallin assumes an importance that still needs to be measured and incorporated into the history of the arts in America. Dallin's *oeuvre* consists of a complicated series of stepping stones toward a worthy goal. His work and the work of his contemporaries, though it may seem out of tune with today's critical notions and shibboleths, deserves far more attention than it has received.

NOTES

RANDOM THOUGHTS OF AN OUTSIDER: MONUMENTAL SCULPTURE IN AMERICA

1. Such earlier examples of sculpture cut into the living rock of a mountain as Thorvaldsen's *Lion of Lucerne* (Fig. 3) or Bartholdi's *Lion of Belfort* were either located directly within the city (Thorvaldsen) or meant to be seen from a vantage point located in a city (Bartholdi).

2. Equally important is yet another religious consideration which involves all of sculpture from c. 1800 on and which therefore would lead too far afield from the purposes of the present catalogue but which should be mentioned. Painting accommodates Protestant ideology in two very different ways: (1) painting executed by painters who happen to be Protestants...e.g., the great majority of Dutch Baroque painting and (2) in its depiction of human destiny and of man's relationship to God and the universe. This latter category is practically limited to the work of only one artist: Rembrandt. Sculpture, as far as I can see, never really achieved a truly Protestant expression and remained bound to its original tradition, which is a Roman Catholic tradition. Even Rodin (who, one must remember, accepted sculpture as a kind of missionary substitute when he realized his lack of vocation to the priesthood) must be seen in this perspective, and probably only with Futurism and the beginnings of a Cubist school of sculpture do we begin to deal with a sculpture that has gone beyond its religious origins.

3. This sculpture by Rush should probably be seen as a native response to Houdon's *Washington* in Richmond. This brings up yet another theme that has been insufficiently explored: the encouragement given to American sculptors by the presence of works imported to America from abroad. Certainly Houdon's *Washington* (arguably one of the greatest works of 18th-century sculpture since it is the only sculpture ever created that combines exaltation of a great individual with democratic ideals of equality) must have exerted considerable pressure on young American artists to equal or excel the first great piece of sculpture to grace American lands. Canova's *Washington* for Raleigh, even though it was destroyed soon after being installed, must have acted as a challenge to Greenough when he set out to carve his great *Washington*, and it would be worth exploring the reactions of American sculptors to later importations, including the *Statue of Liberty* and the sculptures bought during the early stages of the Museum of Fine Arts in Boston and The Metropolitan Museum of Art in New York.

4. It is important to see this phase of American sculpture against the foil of contemporary events on the European scene. Canova's late works as well as almost all of Thorvaldsen's successful sculpture were in the form of large scale or at least life-sized sculptures meant not for any specific location nor dedicated to a specific public educational, moral or propagandistic purpose. Instead these sculptures were intended for private collections where they fulfilled the purpose of ensuring the cultural prestige of their owners. See Ursula Peters, *Kunstlerleben in Rom. Bertel Thorvaldsen (1770-1844). Der dänische Bildhauer und seine deutschen Freunde,* Germanisches Nationalmuseum (Nürnberg, 1991). Crawford and

other American sculptors like him follow much the same pattern.

5. See Victoria Green, "Fabricating the Dream; American World's Fair Sculpture 1876-1915," unpublished doctoral dissertation, Boston University, 1993.

CYRUS E. DALLIN:
HIS SMALL BRONZES AND PLASTERS

Kent Ahrens

i

By the early 20th century, Cyrus E. Dallin had established a reputation as one of America's leading sculptors whose work centered on representing Native Americans—a reputation that he carefully cultivated over the years. Although such notable sculptors as Thomas Crawford, John Quincy Adams Ward, John J. Boyle and Augustus Saint-Gaudens had depicted Native Americans before him, Dallin must be included among the pioneering artists who developed the genre. But in spite of the prominence of Native Americans in his work, Dallin's interests were much more diverse, and included the broad range of subjects usually associated with the leading academic sculptors of the day, such as Saint-Gaudens and Daniel Chester French. Dallin never reached their level of achievement, however: in comparison, his figures seem too static and lack an elusive delicacy of touch in their modeling, and his habitual repetition of forms weakens the quality of his *oeuvre.* Nevertheless, his work reveals him to have been an artist of talent and sensitivity toward his subjects. Besides the large commemorative sculptures that were placed in cities from Salt Lake City to Provincetown, Dallin built a reputation on his accomplished small bronzes and plasters. The last exhibition of Dallin's portable sculpture during his lifetime was more than a half century ago in 1934 at the Boston Art Club, and the Rockwell Museum exhibition brings many objects together perhaps for the first time.

Post-Civil War America saw the development of an interest in small bronzes, an interest that continued until about the 1930s, when they declined in popularity. This was a period during which fortunes were amassed, great houses demanding elaborate decorations were built, and individuals sought private commemorative pieces (as opposed to public monuments honoring national heroes). It was also a period of technical advances in the art of bronze casting, and by the early 20th century the ancient lost-wax process, which would replace sand casting, had been reestablished by companies like Roman Bronze Works and later Gorham Company Founders.[1] The small bronzes of Frederic Remington and other sculptors enjoyed immense popularity. Also, Saint-Gaudens, then French and his generation, discovered that a profit could be made from reduced versions of their public monuments.[2]

Equally important for Dallin's success was the development of high quality plaster casts. The leader in the field was P. P. Caproni and Brother, Boston, a firm established in 1892 by Pietro and Emilio Caproni. Their casts of ancient and modern sculpture helped educate generations of Americans in the arts; they sold their plasters to private individuals, museums and every variety of educational organization from secondary schools to universities, and especially institutions with drawing and modeling classes. By the early 20th century, Caproni sought to include the work of living artists in its large inventory, and Dallin seems to have been one of the first artists with whom the firm developed an extensive working relationship.[3]

ii

Although the Vasarian details of Dallin's childhood and early training as a sculptor vary with the telling, there are recurrent elements in these accounts.[4] His parents, Thomas Dallin and Jane Hamer, who had met during one of the Mormon emigrations from England to the American West, settled in Springville, Utah Territory, following their marriage.[5] Cyrus was born in November 1861. The large family was poor, and much of Cyrus's time was occupied by the odd jobs and chores that engaged young men on the frontier. Still there was time to enjoy idle moments. His young companions were drawn not only from among the townspeople but also the Ute and Piute, who roamed freely through the territory. From Native Americans he learned such skills as archery, and he developed an early appreciation for the integrity of their designs and sense of beauty: "'...The Indian encampments...were always places of beauty. There I saw beautiful colors and combinations of colors which white people are to-day finally adopting....'"[6] He later recalled that from about the age of twelve he sketched and dabbled in clay.[7]

A turning point came in young Dallin's life in 1879, when he was working at the shallow mine operated by his father. Gray-white pliable clay was taken from the mine, and a Mr. Blanchard was so impressed by the two ideal heads that Cyrus modeled that he helped him secure the funds to travel east to study in Boston.[8]

There Dallin apprenticed with Truman H. Bartlett, who was known as much for his writing as for his sculpture. Bartlett is viewed unfavorably in Dallin literature for allegedly threatening Dallin's *Paul Revere* commission by attacking the artist's youth and the design itself.[9] However, the apprenticeship was probably fortuitous for Dallin. Bartlett had studied with the noted French animal sculptor Emmanuel Frémiet and had spent more than a decade in Europe, where his son Paul Wayland Bartlett was studying in Paris. And as Michael Shapiro points out, he was one of the first artists in America to advocate a revival of the process of lost-wax casting, which would later become important to Dallin's work.[10]

Bartlett's letter of January 1880 to Blanchard reveals a sympathy for young artists:

> The best course to pursue is to send him [Dallin] where he can study & where it can be found out if he has the material in him to make something.... A boy of this kind in France is taken up by the town or country & sent to Paris & supported there until he can earn something.... I will see that he is well taken care of....[11]

In June Bartlett wrote Thomas Dallin that Cyrus was "...getting on splendidly...," and added that he would not push him to continuous work until he was more acclimated.[12] But by October Dallin was kept busy enough to write home that he worked in the evenings until ten o'clock in Mr. Bartlett's night school.[13]

During his first year in Boston, Dallin was dependent on funds from home, and he was forced to live on a meager income. With Bartlett's support, in 1880 he modeled a panther that he hoped to sell as terra-cotta casts back home. Casts of the *Algerian Panther*

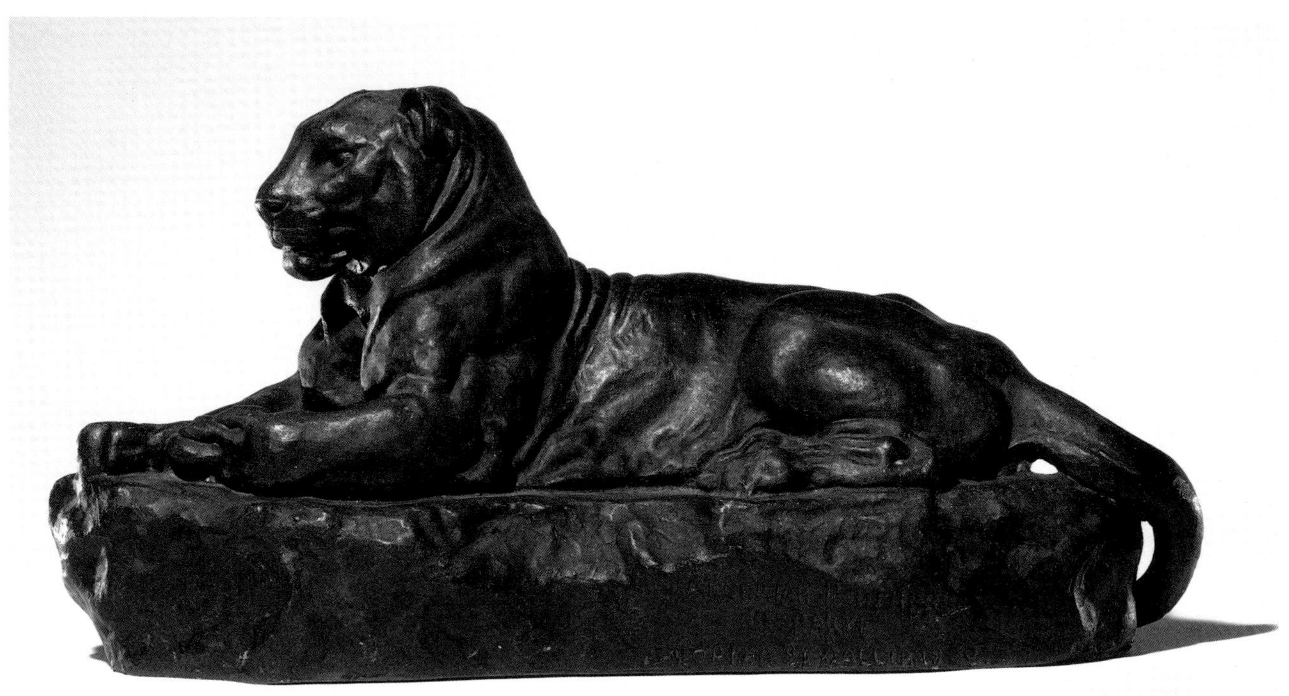

No. 1. Dallin. *Algerian Panther*. Courtesy Museum of Fine Arts, Boston.

(No. 1) were made in a press mold, probably with several parts. On the side Dallin inscribed: *ALGERIAN PANTHER / BY BARYE / COPIED BY DALLIN 1880.*[14] Dallin carefully imitated the articulation of the musculature in his model, which Paula Kozol identified as Antoine-Louis Barye's *Panther of Tunis* (1840).[15]

By the spring of 1881 Bartlett was becoming concerned that Dallin should find a means of supporting himself and secured him a position working for a terra-cotta company.[16] However, perhaps due to ill health, Dallin moved in the fall to Quincy, where he worked for over a year with Sidney H. Morse. By the spring of 1883 Dallin had taken a studio and had become involved with his first model for *Paul Revere.*[17]

In 1882 there had been an open competition in Boston for a bronze equestrian figure of Paul Revere. After two inconclusive competitions, which Dallin won without being awarded the commission, he finally prevailed.[18] In 1885 he signed an agreement with the Committee on the "Paul Revere" Statue (this agreement was extended twice, until 1891).[19] But public opinion cooled to the monument, and funding through proposed subscriptions and contributions failed to materialize. Nevertheless, Dallin persisted in his attempts to secure fulfillment of the agreement and to improve his design. His appeal for support to Augustus Saint-Gaudens brought a reserved response. Saint-Gaudens felt that the horse showed promise, but that the figure was weak. He concluded, "...what I have stated about your work is exactly what I think and it would not be fair to the gentlemen you mention, the public, or myself, should I commit myself to approval of a part of your work that does not

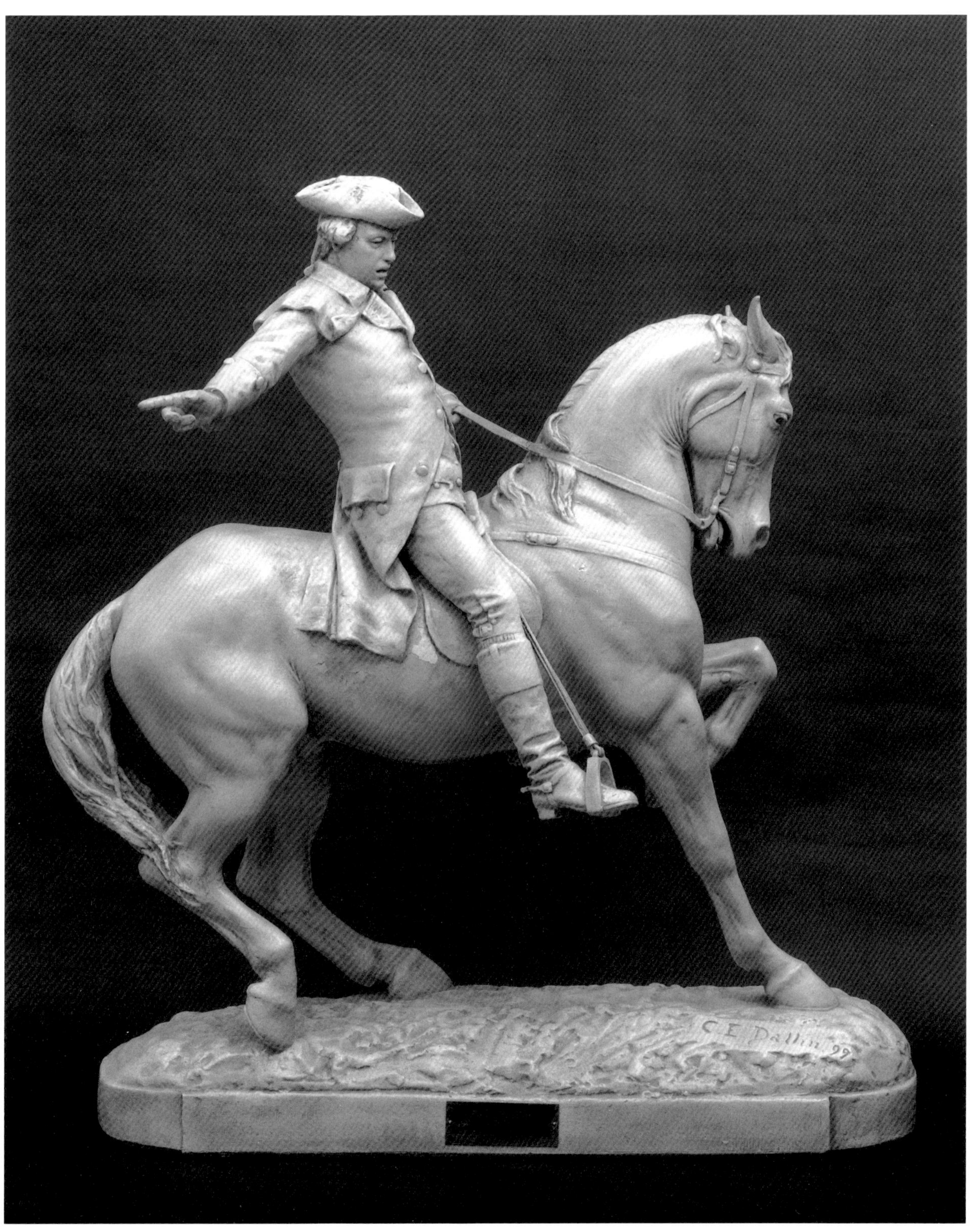

Fig. 7. Dallin. *Paul Revere*. 1899. Plaster. Courtesy Museum of Church History and Art.

satisfy me."[20] Dallin's *oeuvre* reveals an unmistakable influence from Saint-Gaudens (and Daniel Chester French), and on several occasions the younger artist turned to the older for assistance.[21]

In 1899 the Boston Fine Arts Commission approved Dallin's latest design for the Revere monument (Fig. 7), and another fruitless attempt was made to move the project forward.[22] This version of the subject, which was popularized by the P. P. Caproni and Brother plaster cast, was not put into bronze until the Museum of Fine Arts recently authorized a limited casting (No. 46).[23] Dallin's difficulty in modeling sculptural groups in easy motion is perhaps nowhere more evident than in his numerous revisions of *Paul Revere,* but in this version he achieved his most successful solution.

iii

During the mid-19th century, American sculptors followed the path of Horatio Greenough and Hiram Powers to Italy, where master carvers turned their clay models into smoothly finished marbles influenced less by nature than by the neoclassicism of Antonio Canova and Bertel Thorvaldsen. By the 1880s, however, the influence of Paris was rapidly on the rise, and sculptors and painters alike went there to work with the leading academic masters of the day—either at the École des Beaux-Arts or in one of the studios where rigorous examinations were not a prerequisite for entry. The term Beaux-Arts is used to describe the academically oriented tendencies of late 19th- and early 20th-century sculpture, but it must be remembered that rather than a unified style, this was a period of complex diversity and contradiction in the arts. As sculpture and architecture came to be regarded as an ensemble, collaborative working relationships between architects and sculptors reached a new level of importance. Ideal subjects at their best developed poetic haunting qualities as artists sought to express abstract thoughts through human forms, modeled as often as not in a naturalistic manner. Stone remained an important medium, but advances in sand casting and the revival of the art of lost-wax casting gave bronze an increasingly significant place in the arts.[24] Casting in bronze, or even inexpensive plaster, provided an immediate record of the artist's intimate creative process.

The generosity of one of his fiancée's relatives permitted Dallin to study at the Académie Julian in Paris with Henri Chapu from 1888 to 1890. In Paris Dallin regarded François Rude's *The Marseillaise* on the Arc de Triomphe de l'Étoile as the finest example of French sculpture, although he had an "...unbounded admiration for the work and character of his master."[25] Dallin wrote of Chapu, "His bi-weekly visits to the class room were of course the great events of the week, and his entre to the studio was heralded by a hustle and bustle of getting everything into order.... His criticism was always constructively helpful...."[26] Chapu had established his reputation with his life-size *Joan of Arc at Domrémy*, which he first exhibited as a plaster, then as a marble, at the 1870 and 1872 Salons, respectively.[27] The directness of Chapu's naturalistic forms must have made an impression on Dallin. An equally important influence was probably the work by French sculptors who specialized in animals and sporting subjects.

In 1889 Dallin passed the examinations to enter the École des Beaux-Arts, but decided against doing so. A wealthy American dentist, Dr. Thomas W. Evans, conceived the idea of presenting France a statue of Lafayette, and he

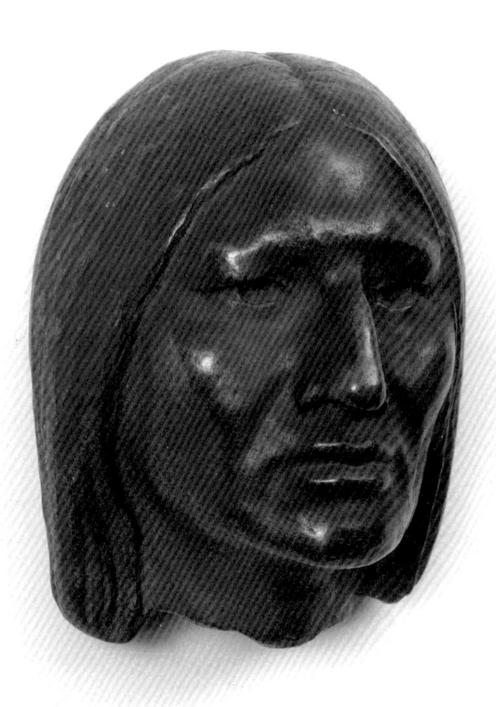

No. 5. Dallin. *Indian Head.*

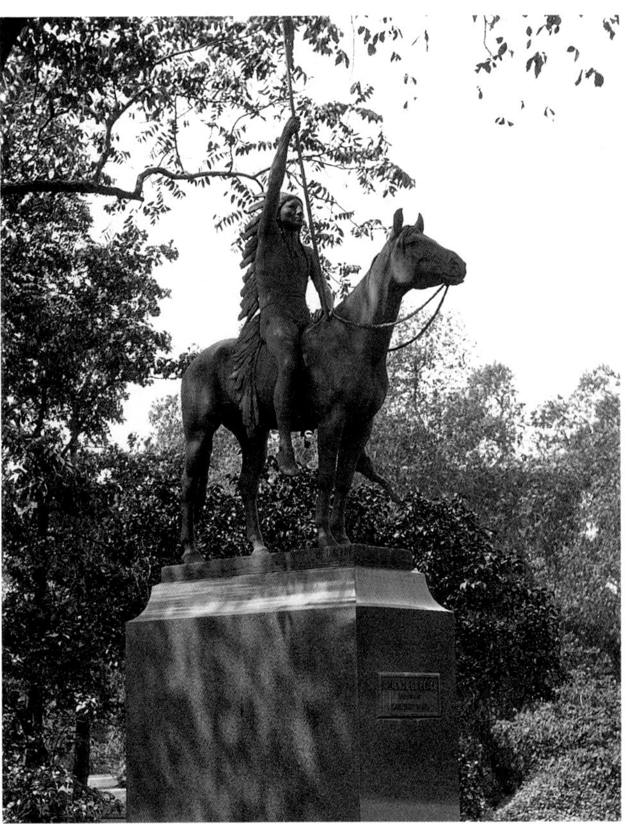

Fig. 8. Dallin. *Signal of Peace.* 1890. Lincoln Park, Chicago. Courtesy Chicago Historical Society.

proposed that Dallin execute the design.[28] The monumental sculpture did not materialize, but Dallin's small bronze was admired by Frémiet at the 1889 Paris Exposition.[29] In designing *Lafayette* (No. 2), Dallin may have kept in mind Thomas Ball's *George Washington* (1858-61), which he greatly admired, although the more advanced design with two hooves raised suggests that Dallin was studying French sources. *Lafayette,* which was cast by Thiebaut, Paris, may have been a unique casting, and it remained in the collection of Dr. Evans.[30]

While frequenting Buffalo Bill's Wild West Show in Paris, Dallin made the acquaintance of Rosa Bonheur, and several charming stories related to her recur in Dallin literature. Besides painting members of the troupe, Bonheur recorded in precisely detailed sketches Native American accessories. Dallin may have modeled his small *Indian Head* (No. 5) during this period.[31] He began the first of his great over life-size Native American equestrians, *Signal of Peace* (Fig. 8).[32]

After Dallin won an honorable mention at the 1890 Salon with a full-size plaster version of *Signal of Peace,* he placed it in storage until 1892, when he had it cast in bronze for the 1893 World's Columbian Exposition. In Chicago, William A. Coffin called it "...one of the best things shown by the Americans."[33] Subsequently, Dallin sold the statue to Judge Lambert Tree, who presented it to the Commissioners of Lincoln Park. For Judge Tree, the sculpture's importance lay in its record of a vanishing people, and in his letter, he left no doubt that he saw the Native Americans as

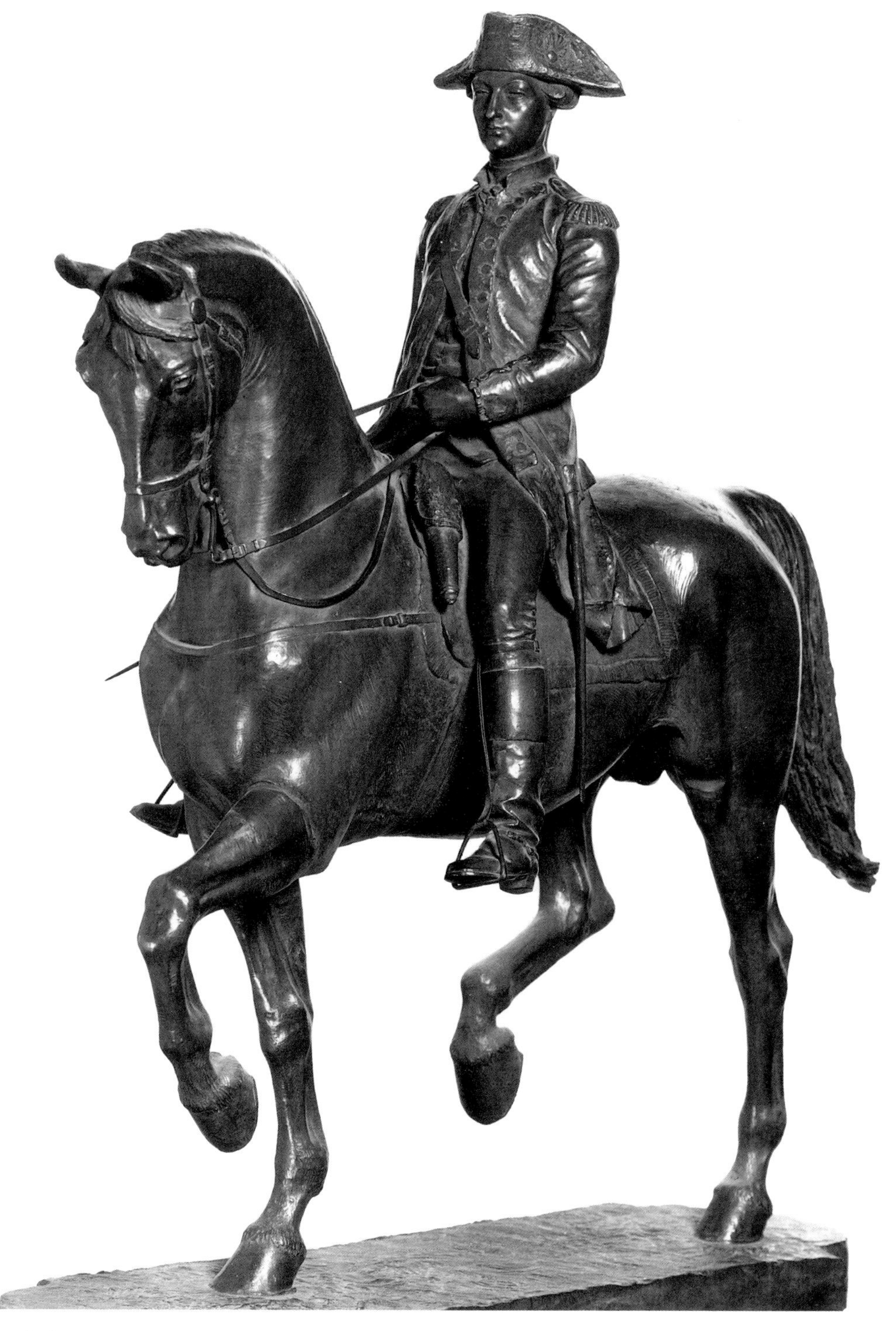

No. 2. Dallin. *Lafayette*.

doomed to extinction: "…it is evident there is no future for them, except as they may exist as a memory in the sculptor's bronze or stone and the painter's canvas."[34]

iv

Dallin returned to Massachusetts from Paris in 1890. He and Vittoria Colonna Murray were married in June 1891, and that summer he took his bride west to Utah. This would be an important trip for the artist.

In Salt Lake City, Dallin undertook portrait busts of the First Presidency of The Church of Jesus Christ of Latter-day Saints—*Wilford Woodruff, George Q. Cannon* (No. 3) and *Joseph F. Smith.* The portraits, which were probably commissioned, represent the three Church leaders in terms of the uncompromising realism that sitters of the day appreciated. Until the busts were recently cast in bronze, they existed only in the form of Dallin's plasters.

Decades of construction reached a climax for The Church of Jesus Christ of Latter-day Saints in 1892, when completion of the exterior of the Salt Lake Temple was celebrated (Fig. 9). As tens of thousands looked on, the capstone was set on April 6, and Dallin's *Angel Moroni* (Fig. 10) was secured in place by an arrangement of iron rods and counterweights.[35] The large Temple figure was not cast but rather made of hammered copper after Dallin's model by W. H. Mullins and Company, Salem, Ohio; it was returned to Salt Lake City for gilding.[36]

Although the Angel Moroni traces its ancestry to the countless sacred and secular figures that appear and reappear in art from the

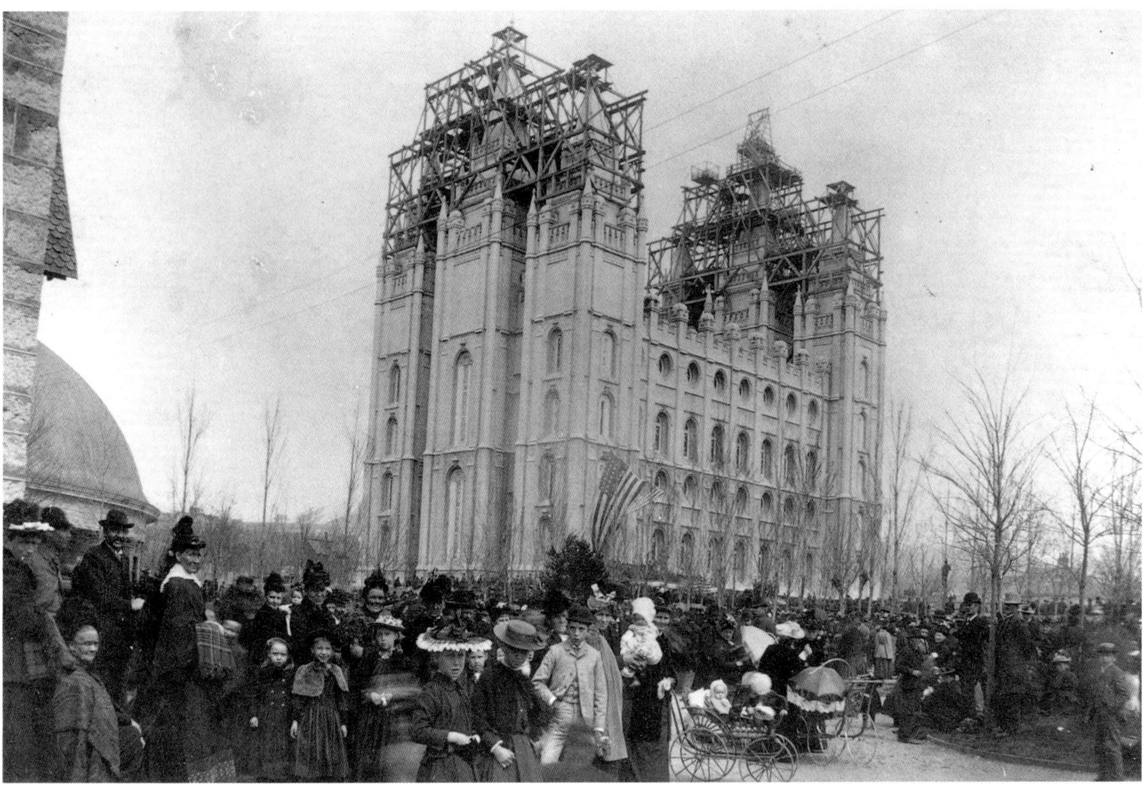

Fig. 9. Installation of Capstone, Salt Lake Temple, April 6, 1892. Courtesy Museum of Church History and Art.

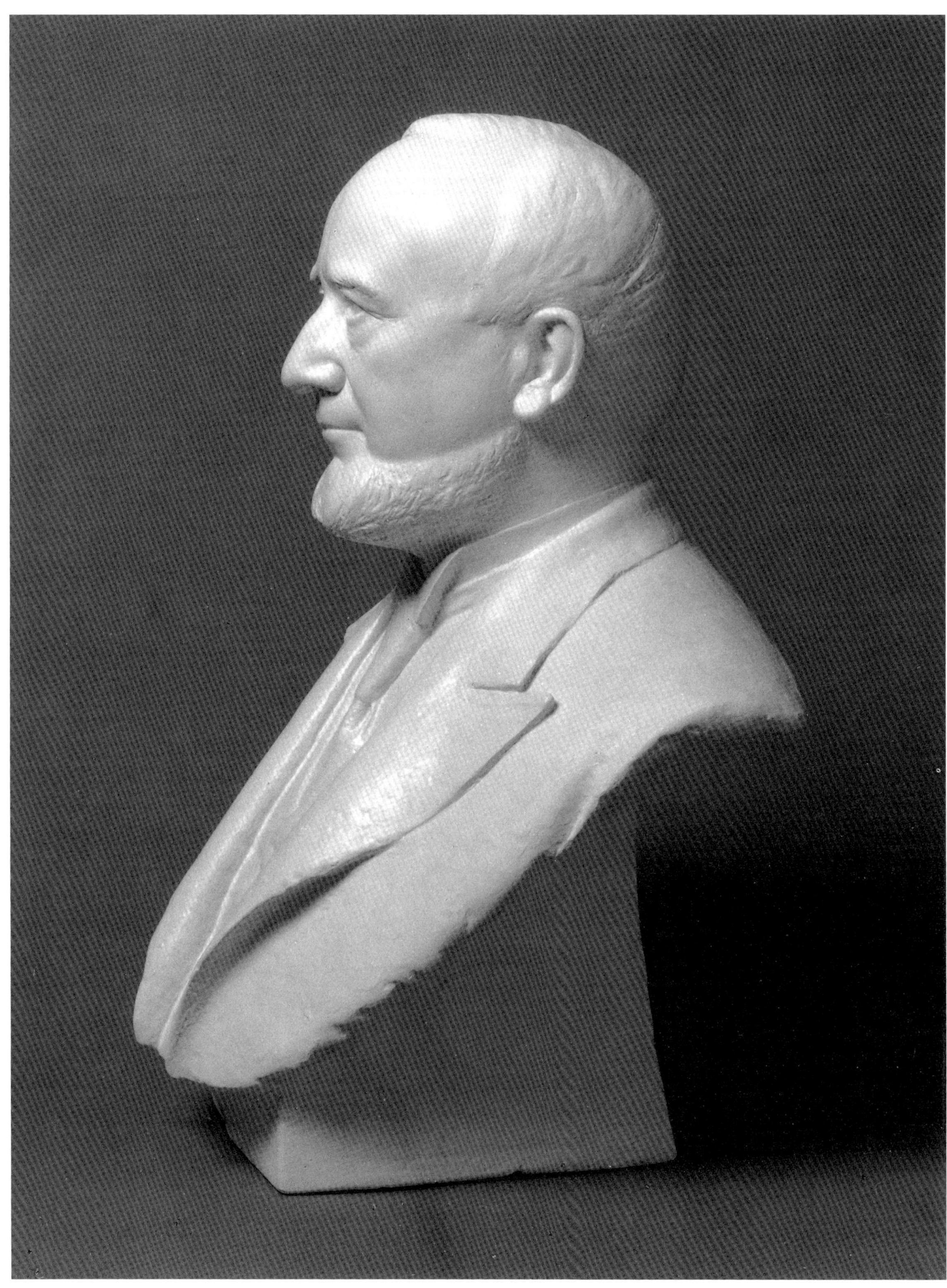

No. 3. Dallin. *President George Q. Cannon.*

Renaissance down through the centuries, Dallin established a new iconographical form for the Church. As President Joseph F. Smith explained to the *Herald,* "...The figure of the angel...is intended to represent, not the Angel Gabriel, sounding the trumpet on resurrection day, but the Angel Maroni, proclaiming the gospel to all the world."[37] President Smith's remarks reflect the importance of Revelations 14:6, which signifies to the Church the modern spreading of the Gospels upon the Earth. According to The Book of Mormon, Moroni was the son of Mormon, who sealed and laid away the records.[38] Joseph Smith recorded that on the night of September 21, 1823, he was visited three times by a herald: "Not only was his robe exceedingly white, but his whole person was glorious beyond description.... He called me by name, and said unto me that he was a messenger sent from the presence of God to me, and that his name was Moroni...."[39] Moroni continued appearing to Smith at regular intervals until September 22, 1827, when he (Moroni) delivered up the plates, which he reclaimed on May 2, 1838.

We know from a drawing by William Weeks that the earlier Temple at Nauvoo, Illinois, which was dedicated in 1846, was surmounted by a flying angel with a trumpet recalling folk art pieces like the *Angel Gabriel* (c. 1800). A watercolor rendering by William W. Ward, Jr. of the proposed new Salt Lake Temple also shows atop either end tower flying figures blowing trumpets.[40] Dallin's robed figure perched upon an orb introduced a new vision of the heavenly messenger. His angel is wingless and offers no clue as to how it came to be so much at ease high upon its lofty perch.

Dallin had a small version of *Moroni* (No. 4) cast in plaster, and it was placed in the Temple c. 1893, when the building was richly

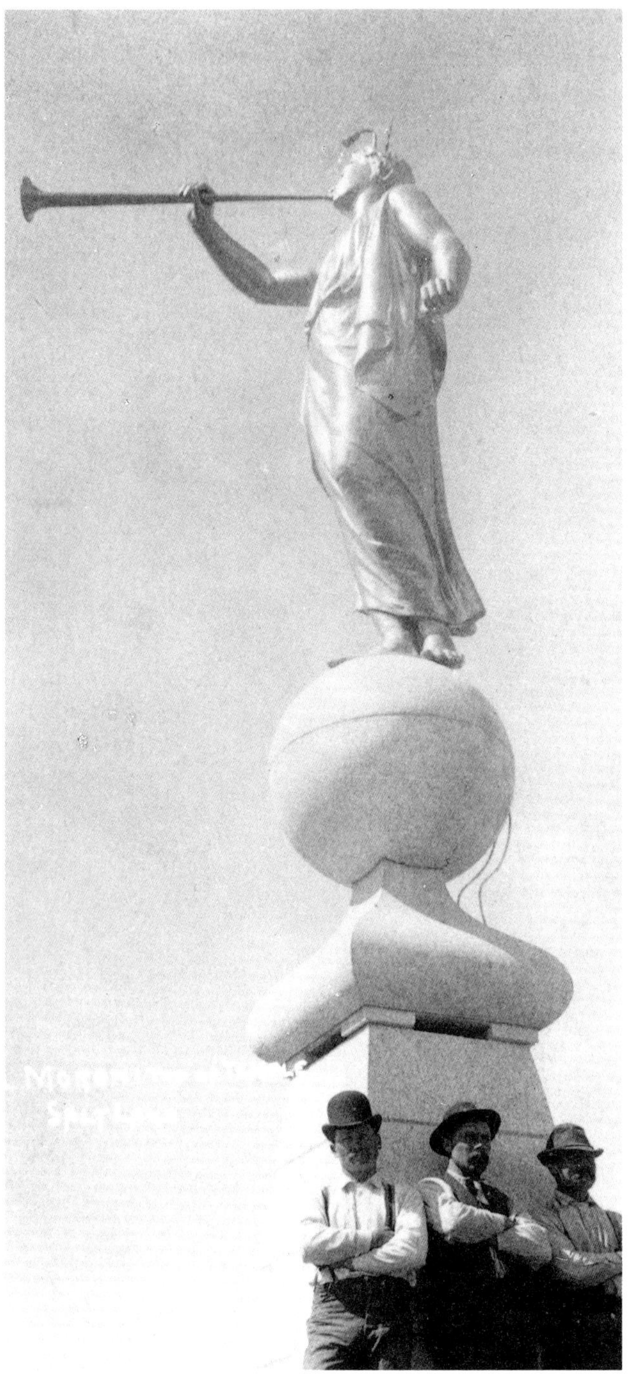

Fig. 10. Workmen with *Angel Moroni*, Salt Lake Temple, Spring 1892. Courtesy Museum of Church History and Art.

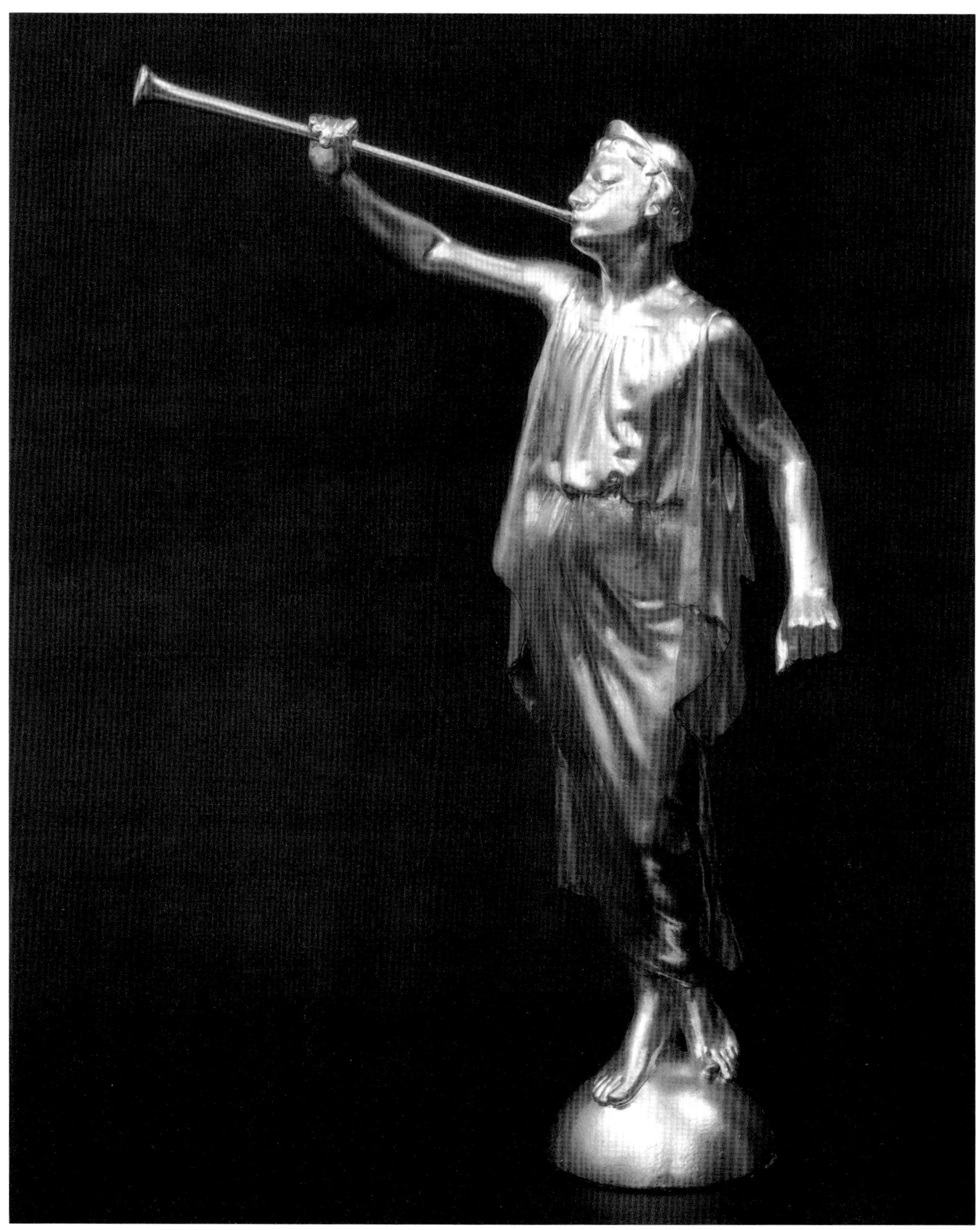

No. 4. Dallin. *Angel Moroni.*

furnished. There the statue remained until recently, and it has not been exhibited elsewhere. Additionally, twelve other copies of the statue were cast in plaster for the twelve apostles of the Church.[41]

Two days after the unveiling of *Moroni* atop the Temple, Dallin signed an agreement on April 8, 1892, with the Brigham Young Memorial Association for a monument dedicated to *Brigham Young and the Pioneers.*[42] Like the *Revere* project, the Salt Lake City monument would cause the artist nearly a decade of frustration; payment was often slow, and the memorial in its final form did not satisfy Dallin. Nevertheless, it remains the most complex of his early designs.

V

In 1893 Dallin was elected to the National Sculpture Society, whose objective reads in part, "...to spread the knowledge of good sculpture; foster the taste for, and encourage the production of, ideal sculpture for the household and museums; promote the decoration of public and other buildings, squares and parks with sculpture of a high class...."[43] The Society's aim to embellish architecture is exemplified by the Library of Congress, which was designed by Smithmeyer and Pelz after the Paris Opera. It is one of the nation's most beautifully executed buildings in the Beaux-Arts style, and an army of artists, including Dallin, contributed to its flawlessly crafted decoration.[44] His *Sir Isaac Newton* is one of sixteen statues representing illustrious men of Western civilization that are set along the rotunda balustrade.[45] Dallin modeled the figure while acting as a substitute instructor for Charles Grafly in Philadelphia.

* * * * *

After studying at the Pennsylvania Academy of the Fine Arts, Grafly went to Paris in 1888—the same year as Dallin—to study also with Chapu. When Grafly again returned to Paris in 1895 to begin his monumental *Vulture of War,* Dallin was hired to teach his classes at the Drexel Institute for an academic year.[46]

In 1891 Anthony J. Drexel had established the Drexel Institute, "...for the promotion of education in art, science, and industry...."[47] The Art Department, which in the 1894-95 academic year became the Department of Fine and Applied Arts, was one of the central divisions of Drexel Institute during its early years, and the first department to offer a four-year course of study.[48] Unfortunately, a catalogue listing Dallin's courses cannot be located for the year in question, 1895-96, although the 1896-97 catalogue again lists Grafly's courses in clay modeling.[49] Presumably these were the same courses that Dallin taught.[50]

Dallin's year in Philadelphia seems to have been exhilarating, and in June 1896 he wrote to Heber Wells, "We are off Saturday for a year abroad.... My star seems distinctly in the ascending, and I shall redouble my efforts to do better work...."[51] The Dallins would remain in Europe for three years while he studied with Jean Dampt, an Art Nouveau sculptor known for his brilliant surfaces.[52] This trip permitted Dallin's style to mature, and the resulting sense of naturalistic form is seen to advantage in the small bronzes and plasters he executed over his remaining career.

Dallin again wrote to Governor Heber Wells from Paris in March 1899 to ask for $1,200 against the Brigham Young Memorial: "...My duties at the Boston Normal Art School begin Monday next, and as I am a special instructor my duties are comparatively light.... I have left my 'Medicine Man' to be put into bronze for the coming Salon and later for the Exposition.... Mr. St. Gaudens was most enthusiastic over the statue, and I believe I shall have a success with it...."[53] The teaching position was the beginning of his long career as an art instructor in Massachusetts, and in 1900 the Dallins purchased a home in Arlington Heights, where they resided the rest of his life.[54]

vi

Dallin's reputation today rests almost entirely upon four Native American subjects: *Signal of Peace* (1890), discussed above, *Medicine Man* (1899), *Protest* (1904), which was not cast in bronze, and *Appeal to the Great Spirit* (1909).

While Dallin was traveling east by train in 1880, he developed a friendship with a group of Native Americans on their way to Washington, and years later he recalled: "...I have never got over that chance four-day contact with those Indians on that trip from Utah to Kansas City. It has influenced my life and my art for half a century.... It was while I was in Paris that I conceived the idea of Indian equestrian groups which have since been completed.... 'The Signal of Peace' was the first...."[55] Apparently the four equestrians were first joined iconographically in print by Alvan Sanborn in his 1909 letter from Paris:

> The "Medicine Man," which is now in Fairmount Park, Philadelphia, is the second of a series of four statues which synthesize in simple and impressive symbols the tragic history and the pathetic destiny of the aborigines of America. The first of the series is: "The Signal of Peace" (now in Lincoln Park, Chicago), a mounted chief, nude, like the Medicine Man, save for moccasins, breech clout and war bonnet, with one hand on the

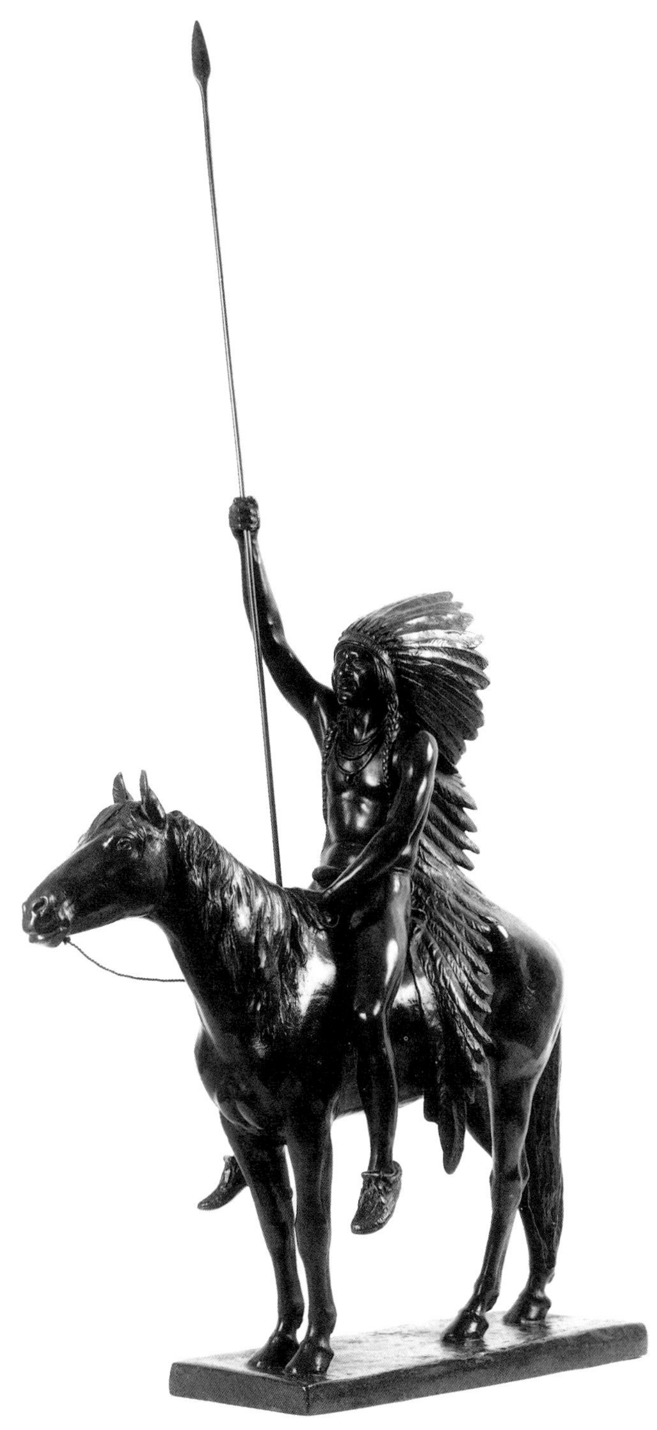

No. 6. Dallin. *Signal of Peace.*

> neck of his mount and the other holding upright a feathered spear as a sign that he yearns for peace. The third is "The Protest" (exhibited at St. Louis in 1904), which represents a chief hurling defiance in the teeth of the superior forces arrayed against his race. The fourth, "The Appeal to the Great Spirit"...is a glorification of the red man's "lost cause." Resistance having proved as vain as the overtures of peace and the vaticinations of the prophet, there is nothing left for him but "an appeal to the higher court."[56]

M. Stannard May was next to summarize the four equestrians together in 1912, and the Museum of Fine Arts followed suit in 1913.[57] Every article of any length after that repeated the account of Dallin's "cycle," and contemporary historians have reinforced these accounts in their writing.[58]

The volume of surviving clippings indicates that Dallin was rather sophisticated in dealing with the press, and one is left to wonder why he made no mention of his intention to produce a cycle of four equestrians until after the fourth—*Appeal to the Great Spirit*—was cast. Certainly, the literature does not take into account such later work as the *Scout* in Kansas City or *On the Warpath* (No.15), which was cast in several sizes.[59] It may be that the information the artist supplied Sanborn in Paris simply represented the evolution of his thinking up to that point—information that, as it became formalized in print, Dallin realized he

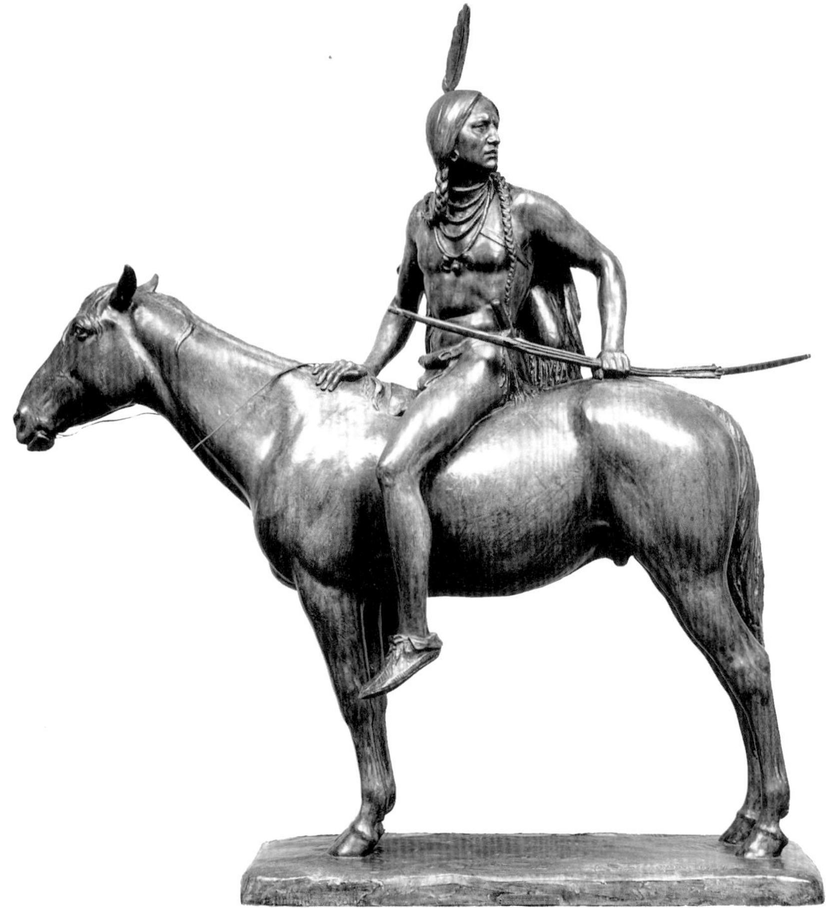

No. 15. Dallin. *On the Warpath.*

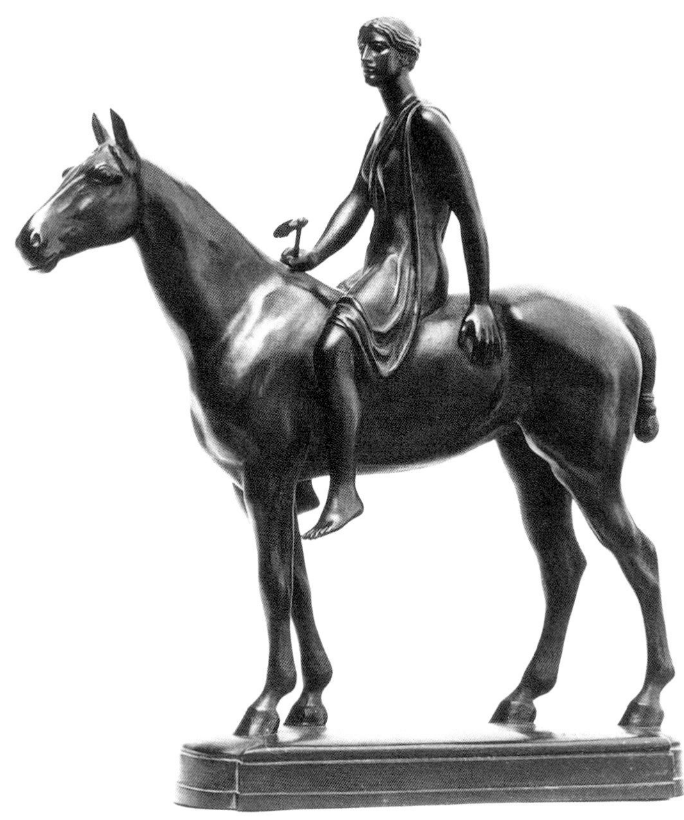

Fig. 11. Louis Tuaillon. *Amazon*. c. 1895. Bayerische Staatsgemäldesammlungen, München.

could capitalize on in marketing his art.

Like such sculptors as Solon Borglum and James Earle Fraser, Dallin's early contact with Native Americans in the West left him with a profound respect for their cultures (perhaps Fraser's *End of the Trail* and Dallin's *Appeal to the Great Spirit* most eloquently express the Native American's struggle). Dallin maintained a speaking acquaintance with Native Americans in Utah, and he was an eloquent spokesman for them.[60] When he was in Kansas City in 1915 negotiating the shipment of the *Scout,* he commented, "I have naturally given more of my time and interest to the picturing of the Indian during my artistic career because of my belief in the race...."[61] He told one newspaperman:

> ...As a child, I could never understand the bullying cowboys. I hated them.... The Indians were uniformly gentle.... Our civilization is going for a fall unless it brings us, as real art brings us, into harmony with the universe. Now, the Indian was closer to nature than we are. Therein is the great fundamental difference between his art and most of ours. His attitude was reverential, a prayer to the Great Spirit, an expression of the holy things of his life. His art thus teaches the fundamental principles of harmony.... Now what can we do to help repair the damage that the white man has done? Most of it is irreparable....[62]

Elsewhere he remarked, "'You have heard that the Indians were warlike and had to be cleared

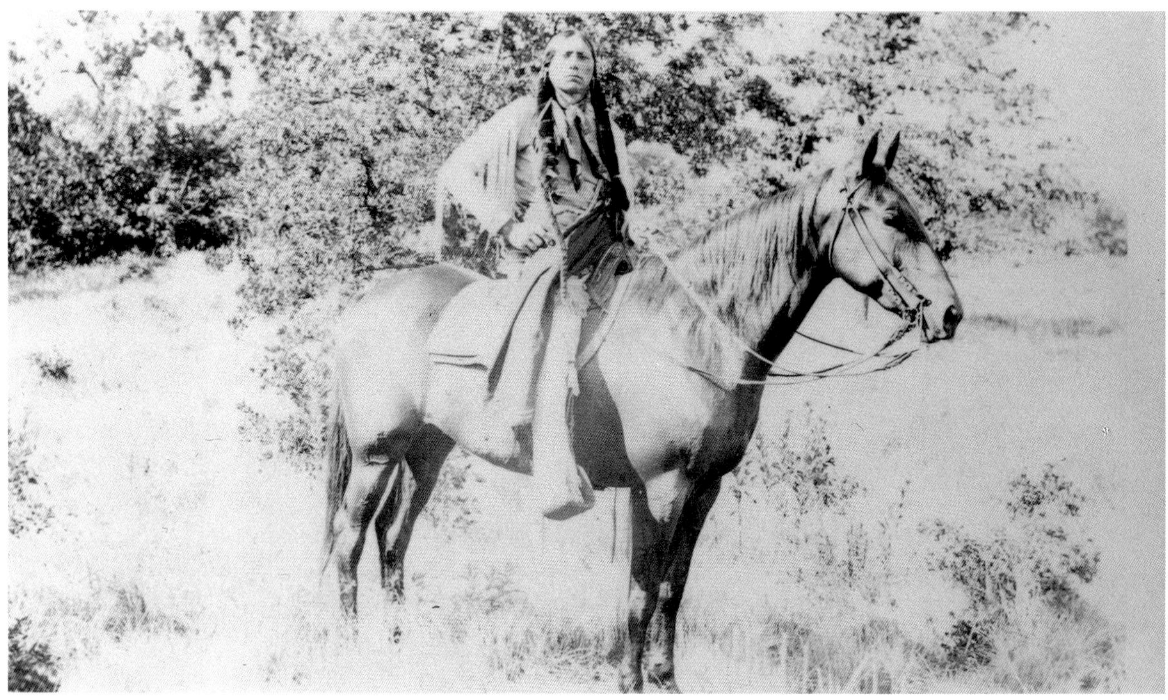

Fig. 12. Quannah Parker, Kwahadi Comanche Chief. Buffalo Bill Historical Center, Cody, Wyoming. Vincent Mercaldo Collection.

from the prairies in order to insure the safety of the white pioneers.... The truth is that we cheated the Indians....'"[63] Paradoxically, he was a son of settlers, and he felt westward expansion was justified: "'I do not blame the white man for taking the Indian's lands.... That was the white man's privilege....'"[64]

Pictorial records of the inhabitants of the Americas can be traced back to the early age of exploration. Gustavus Hesselius's portraits and later Benjamin West's great history paintings established the Native American in 18th-century art. During the course of the 19th century, the subject of the Native American became a significant if minor theme for portraitists, history painters and sculptors. While scientific discovery may have increasingly captured the energies of 19th-century thought, the mantle of romanticism had fallen heavily across the Western world and would not readily be lifted. A persistent theme of romanticism was the exotic, and American and European artists traveled the world in search of wonder. The subject of the Native American—with due respect to George Catlin's emphasis on the personal experience and a degree of scientific accuracy—was grounded in the romantic fascination with the exotic. From this perspective, it is not surprising that there should be such striking points of comparison as there are between Dallin's Native American equestrians and European sculpture like, for example, Louis Tuaillon's *Amazon* (Fig. 11) (the paradox is that for Dallin the Native American was not an exotic subject, but an integral part of his childhood experience, although he would capitalize on it). While it is an oversimplification, 19th-century depictions of Native Americans fall into several broad categories: noble savages, guileless interpreters of truth; innocent children of the wilderness made whole (or destroyed, as the case may be) by conversion to Christianity; self-sufficient and wise inhabitants of the wilderness; dignified remnants of a disappearing civilization; converts to Anglo-European customs; brutal savages; enemies of settlers; common drunks; pathetic survivors doomed to extinction.

Dallin's high regard for Native Americans and his sympathy for the abuses they suffered no doubt influenced his sculpture—especially the public monuments. Other artists surpassed Dallin in recording Native Americans and their mounts in action, Frederic Remington and Alexander Phimister Proctor among them. Dallin's association with Native Americans never produced anything like the unique series of portrait reliefs created by Olin Warner during his trip to the Northwest Territory in the 1880s. Neither do Dallin's surfaces possess the facile decorative quality of contemporaries like Adolph Weinman and Charles H. Humphriss, nor the grace of Hermon Atkins MacNeil. Nevertheless, Dallin produced a series of equestrian figures that are timeless in their monumentality. Dallin was sensitive to the har-

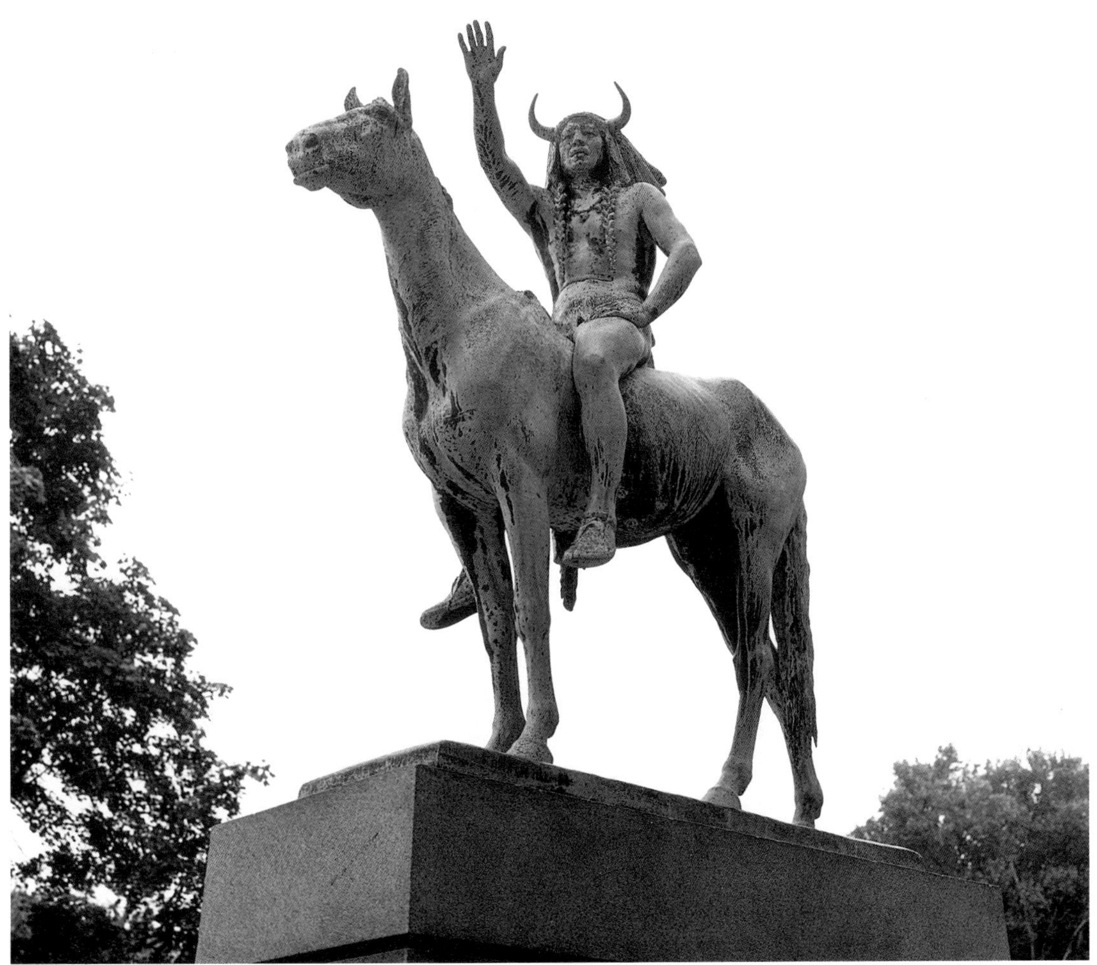

Fig. 13. Dallin. *The Medicine Man*. 1899. East Fairmont Park, Philadelphia. Courtesy Fairmount Park Art Association. Photographer Howard Brunner.

mony that exists between Native Americans, their animal relatives and the Mother Earth; in this context, Dallin's horses do not stand statically, but as conduits of nature's energies. Rather than relying on specific detail, he preferred to generalize within the boundaries of Northern Plains accessories.[65] While he worked his surfaces to suggest texture, the flickering play of light never surpasses the importance of form and structure. Most turn-of-the-century artists who specialized in the West maintained elaborate studio props, but old photographs reveal no such paraphernalia in his studio. Dallin probably relied instead on photography, in which there is a still and timeless quality like that of his sculpture (Fig. 12).[66]

* * * * *

Europeans responded favorably to Dallin's *Medicine Man* (Fig.13) when he exhibited it at the Paris Salon in 1899 and at the Exposition in 1900; one offer from Austria to purchase the bronze fell through only after it was learned that Dallin was offering a second cast.[67] Lorado Taft called it the best work Dallin had yet produced, and in his influential book, *The History of American Sculpture,* he elaborated his praise.[68] Wayne Craven more recently recognized in the *Medicine Man* the establishment of a new equestrian genre—previously limited in American art almost exclusively to military heroes—combined with a sense of the monumental that avoided a reliance on the picturesque.[69]

Dallin may have approached Fairmount Park Art Association in an effort to sell the *Medicine Man* as early as 1898, but it was not purchased until 1901, when it was placed on Strawberry Hill.[70] At the formal presentation ceremonies, a plaster cast was presented for the Mayor of Philadelphia's acceptance. There followed a lecture, "Who Was the Medicine Man?" by Francis La Flesche, himself a Native American scholar of note, who explained the profound spiritual role of the Men of Mystery (so-called Medicine Men) in preserving the rites and ceremonies of the tribe. La Flesche remarked, "...in the serious expression, the dignified bearing, the strength of pose, I recognize [in the sculpture] the character of the true Medicine Man...he who was the mediator between his people and the great Spirit...."[71]

The Universal Exposition of 1904 in Saint Louis celebrated the 19th-century assumption that civilization itself was a progressive development. In the large anthropological section, primitive peoples and their artifacts were assembled from all over the world, in the certainty that they would soon vanish forever.[72] Following the tradition established by the Columbian Exposition (1893), the Saint Louis fair consisted of a rich assortment of Beaux-Arts architecture and monumental sculpture constructed of impermanent materials. Karl Bitter was responsible for the unity of the sculptural program. After Bitter approved an artist's model, it would be enlarged in staff by the army of assistants he employed at his workshop in New Jersey, from which the sculpture was shipped West.[73]

Dallin exhibited two monumental figures in staff at the Saint Louis fair—*Pere Marquette,* which is known only from photographs, and *Sioux Chief* (Fig. 14), or the *Protest* as it is more commonly titled.[74] As Bitter reported, Dallin's *Sioux Chief* formed an iconographical unity with other sculpture. Edward Clark Potter's *De Soto* and Alexander Phimister Proctor's *Louis Joliet* were equestrian figures placed in front of the Varied Industries and Manufactures buildings, respectively, as appro-

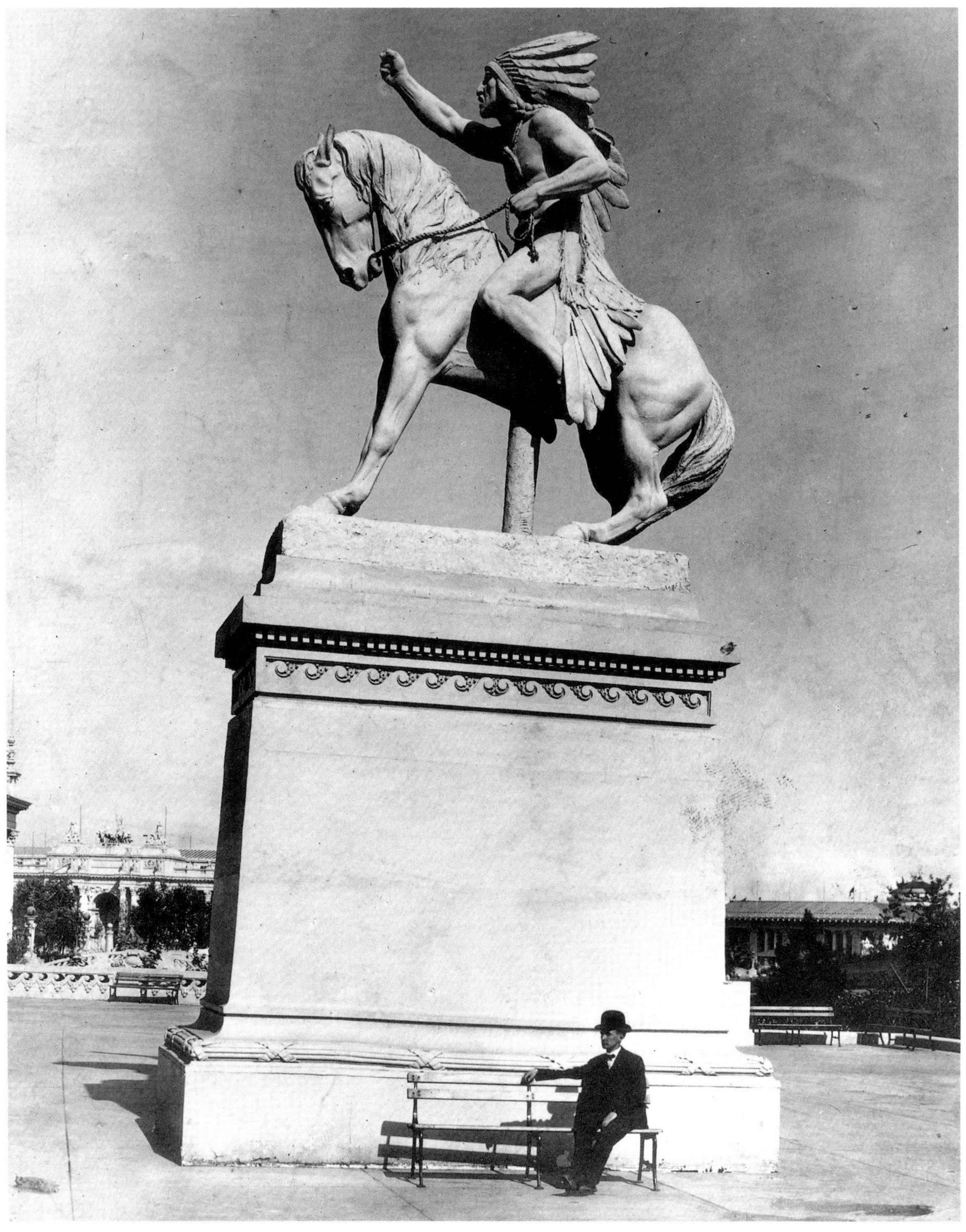

Fig. 14. Dallin. *Protest: The Sioux Chief* (at the 1904 World's Fair). Missouri Historical Society.

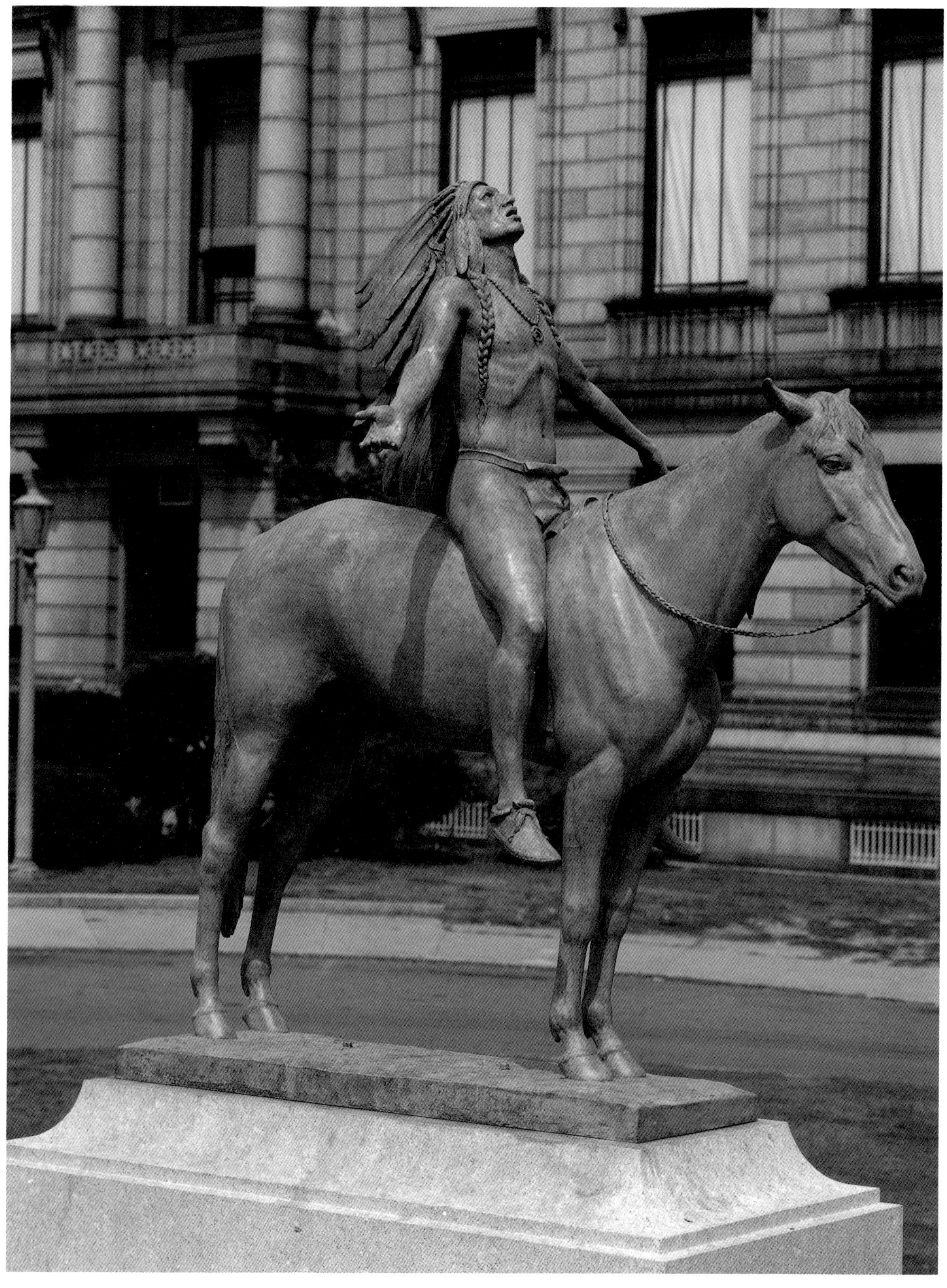

Fig. 15. Dallin. *Appeal to the Great Spirit*. 1909. Gift of Peter C. Brooks and Others. Courtesy Museum of Fine Arts, Boston.

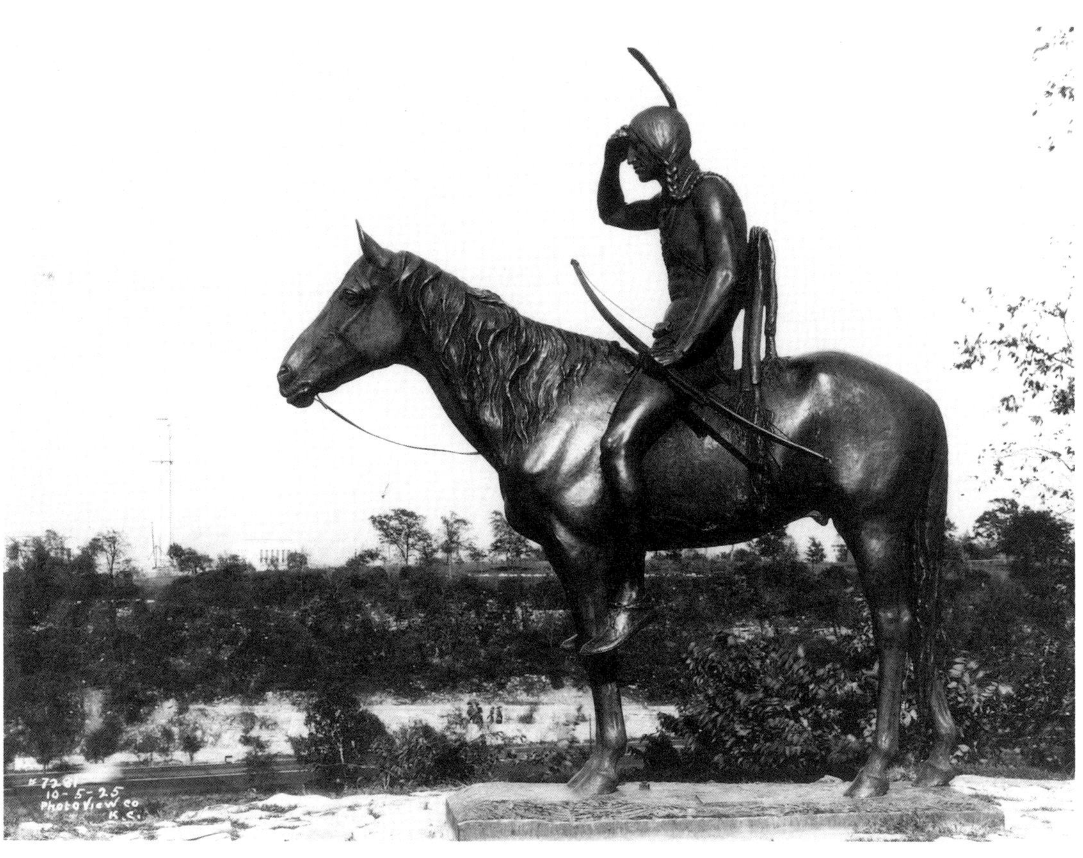

Fig. 16. Dallin. *The Scout*. 1914. Penn Valley Park, Kansas City, Missouri. Courtesy Parks and Recreation.

priate symbols of the first two nations associated with the land forming the Louisiana Purchase. Then, near Festival Hall were James Earle Fraser's *Cherokee Chief* and Dallin's *Sioux Chief,* "...as representatives of the people from whom this region was taken...."[75] On the eastern side of the Sunken Garden, the Native American's anticipated demise was depicted by Adolph Weinman's *The Destiny of the Redman,* which "...spoke of his pathetic end."[76]

It was Dallin's fourth equestrian statue that firmly secured his reputation. After a plaster version of Dallin's now-famous *Appeal to the Great Spirit* was exhibited in Baltimore in 1908, it was cast in bronze by Jaboeuf & Rouard Fondeurs, Paris, where it won a medal at the 1909 Salon.[77] Since it was too large to fit inside, it was exhibited outside of the National Academy of Design in 1911, then placed on a temporary pedestal in front of the Museum of Fine Arts, Boston.[78] The Art Commission gave its early approval of the statue, and a group of artists and architects joined together with the Metropolitan Improvement League to raise funds by subscription. But progress was slow, and other cities—especially Kansas City—expressed interest in the statue. Finally Peter C. Brooks gave a large portion of the necessary funds, and the bronze was secured for Boston. Various sites were suggested before the front of the Museum was agreed upon (Fig. 15).[79]

Dallin wrote of the *Appeal to the Great Spirit,* "...It has frequently been misinterpreted.... after the Indian had offered his signal of peace...and it had been rejected, I wanted

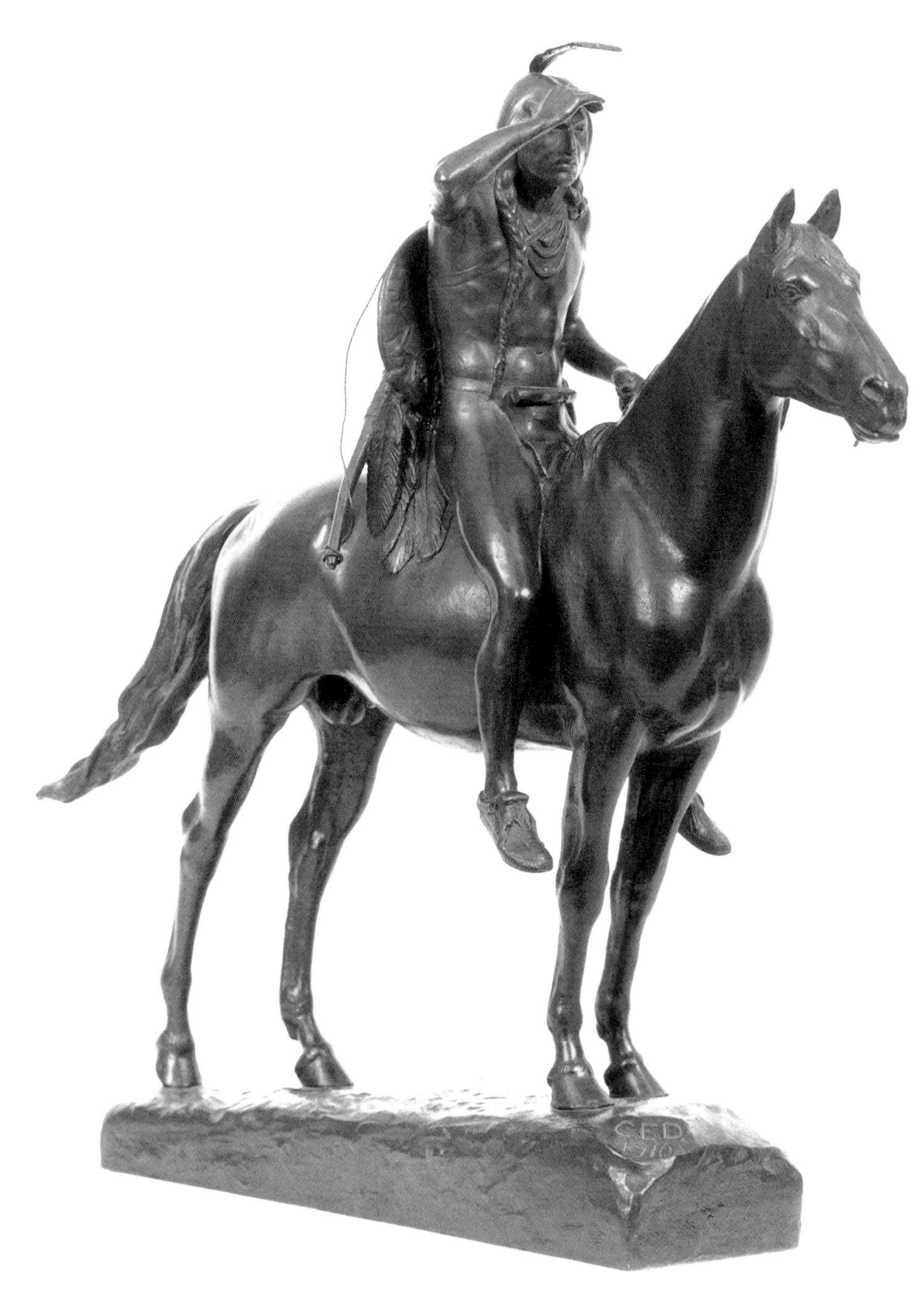

No. 14. Dallin. *The Scout.* From the Collection of Gilcrease Museum, Tulsa.

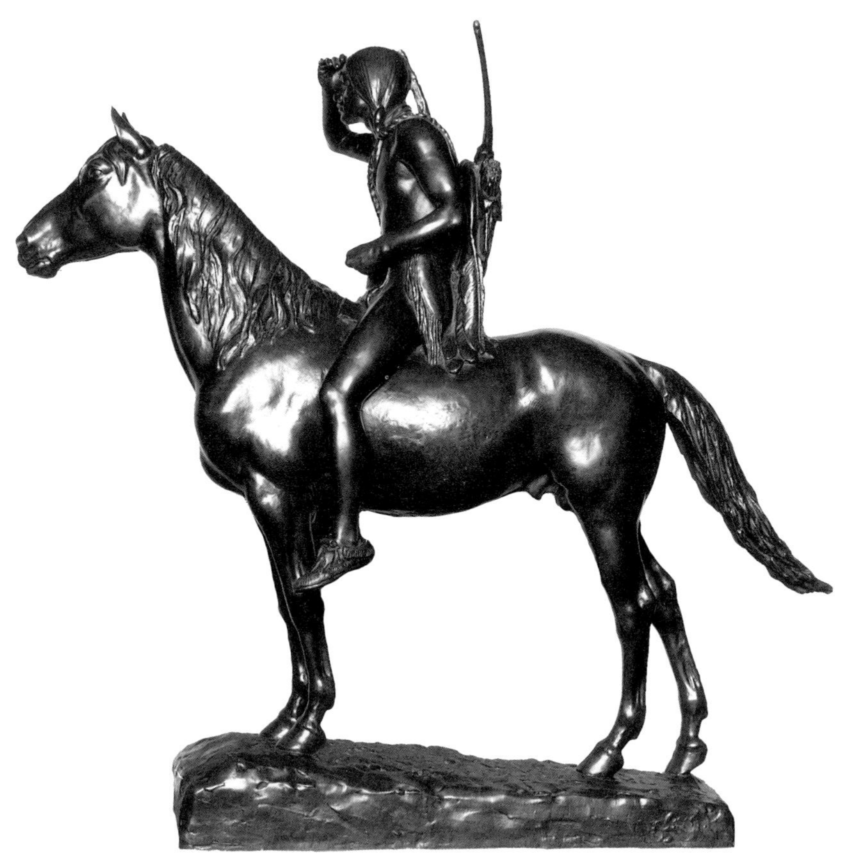

No. 13. *The Scout.*

to show the Indian as making a final appeal to the Great Spirit for peace with the white man."[80] In 1912 Dallin filed a copyright on the large bronze, but by the 1920s it had become such a popularly reproduced image that he went to court in unsuccessful suits against alleged copyright violations.[81] Ironically, the *Appeal to the Great Spirit* became the inspiration for poetry and musical lyrics that more often than not conveyed a specifically Christian sentimentality—not the Native American's view of the universe.[82]

* * * * *

The Scout (Fig. 16), Dallin's fifth over life-size Native American equestrian, has a history similar to its predecessors. Following its exhibition at the Panama-Pacific Exposition (1915) in San Francisco, it was shipped to Kansas City, where, thanks to the enthusiasm of attorney Delbert J. Hall, a public subscription was launched, and funds were finally raised to purchase the bronze.[83] Interpretations vary widely in print, but perhaps Frank Titus best summed up the statue's symbolism: "This statue is in truth an epitome in miniature of the transformation of the great territory west of the Missouri River from a state of nature to a rich

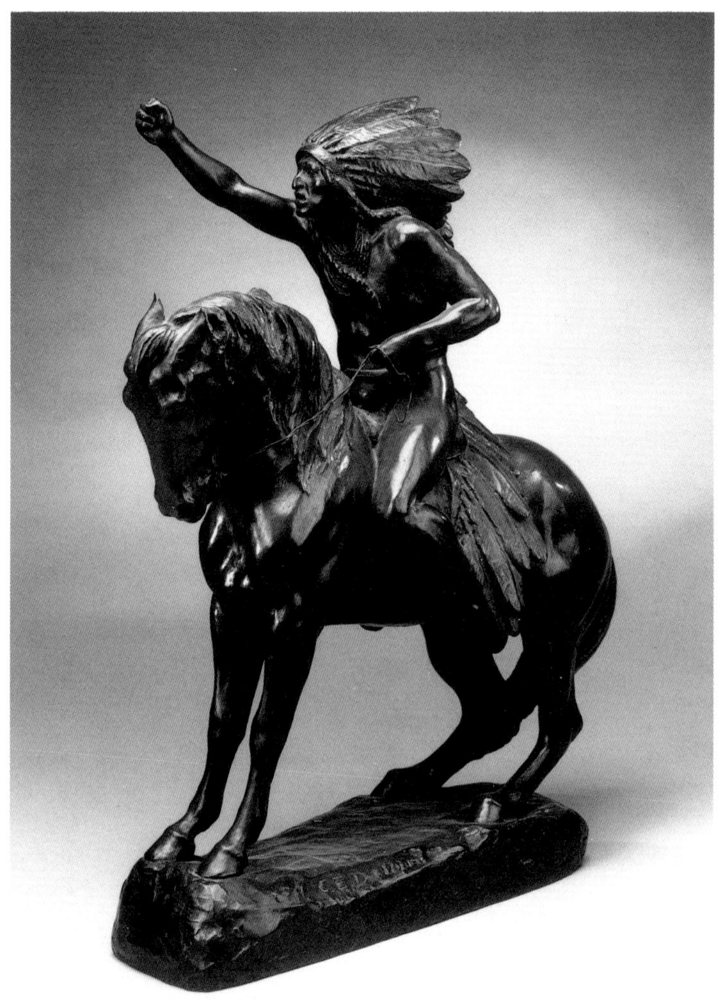

No. 8. Dallin. *Protest.*

and populous empire...." It marked "...an epochal national era," he continued.[84] Dallin wrote in 1917, "...This is the last of my equestrian Indians and technically I consider it my best."[85] It is difficult to disagree with the artist: the *Scout* is handsomely modeled and proportioned, with a remarkable sense of vitality.

* * * * *

Except for the *Protest*, the equestrians under discussion were apparently put into bronze by Dallin at his own expense on the speculation that he would be able to sell them, and that he would be able to capitalize further by the sale of reduced versions. Although Dallin relied upon the excellence of French foundries, he turned increasingly to American companies for his small bronzes—The Henry-Bonnard Bronze Company, Roman Bronze Works and Gorham Company Founders. In some instances Dallin would have one foundry, then another, cast a subject; two examples are the *Medicine Man* (No. 7), which was first cast by Gruet Jeune Fondeur, Paris, then Roman Bronze and Gorham, both of which also cast the *Protest* (No. 8).[86] In the case of the *Signal of Peace* (No. 6), which was probably the first

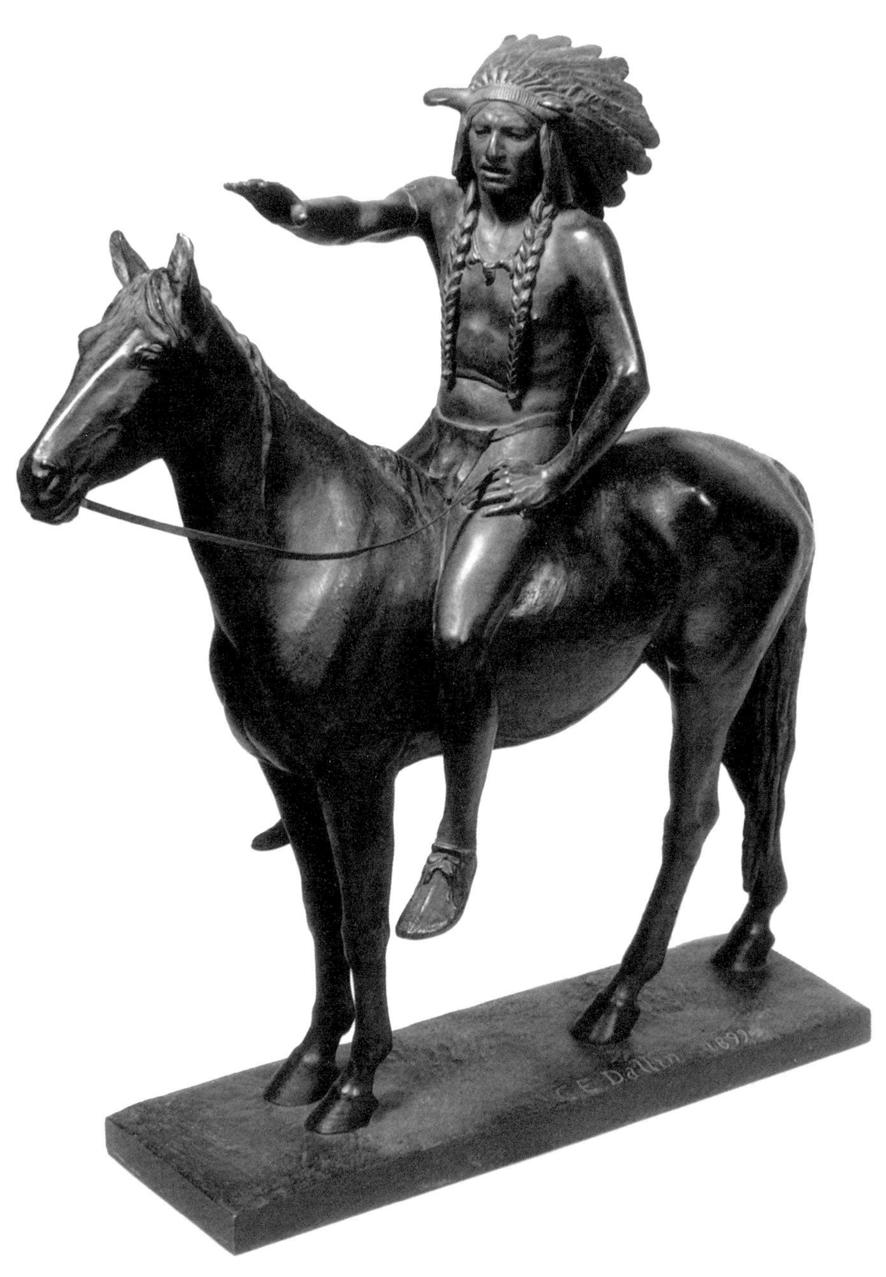

No. 7. Dallin. *Medicine Man*.

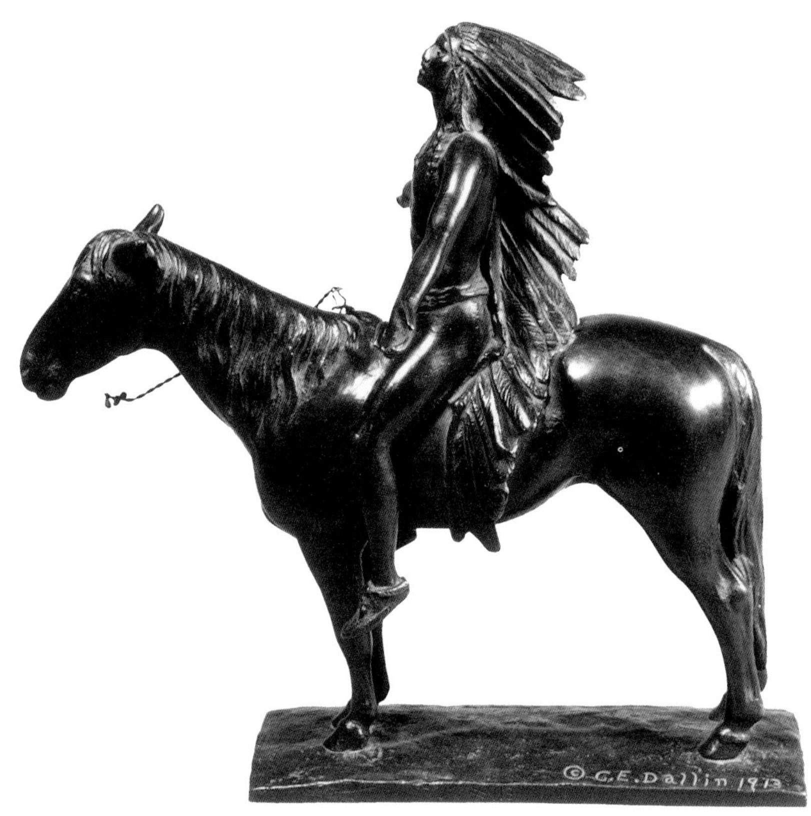

No. 9. Dallin. *Appeal to the Great Spirit.*

equestrian to be modeled, it was not cast in bronze until the 1920s.[87] Likewise, the reduced versions of the *Scout* (Nos. 13 and 14), which differ in detail from the Kansas City sculpture, were not cast in bronze for a number of years after being modeled.[88]

A discussion of the various versions of the *Appeal to the Great Spirit* is instructive. Dallin transferred ownership of the large statue to the Museum of Fine Arts in 1912 for the sum of $12,000. He reserved, "...however, to myself the right to make and sell reproductions...not in any instance to exceed three feet in their greatest dimension...."[89] During Dallin's life, Gorham cast the subject in three sizes (Nos. 9, 10 and 11), each identified by the foundry's unique identification system:

QAPU	36"	9 cast.
QPN	20"	107 cast.
QXC	9"	283 cast.

Dallin usually received a royalty when his small bronzes were sold by Gorham, but the method of their distribution could vary.[90]

Dartmouth College's cast of the *Appeal to the Great Spirit* must be counted among Dallin's finest achievements. It is in excellent condition, having stood virtually undisturbed in Baker Library since it was given to Dartmouth in the 1920s. Sculptures in this general size permitted the artist to develop forms fully, then enrich the surfaces to suggest texture and detail in the accessories. Dallin must have appreciated the rich patina produced by Gorham—reflected by both the Dartmouth

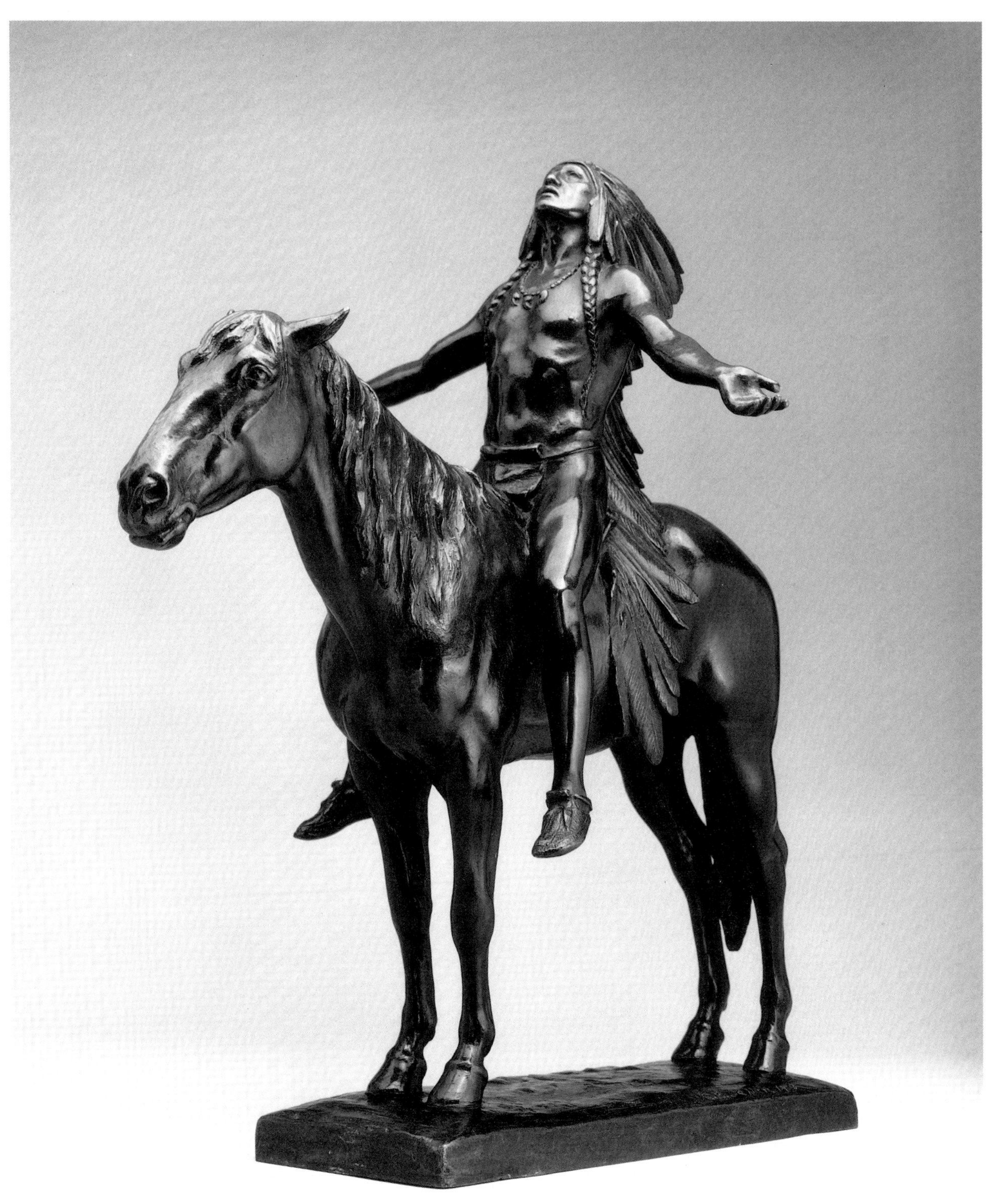

No. 10. Dallin. *Appeal to the Great Spirit*.

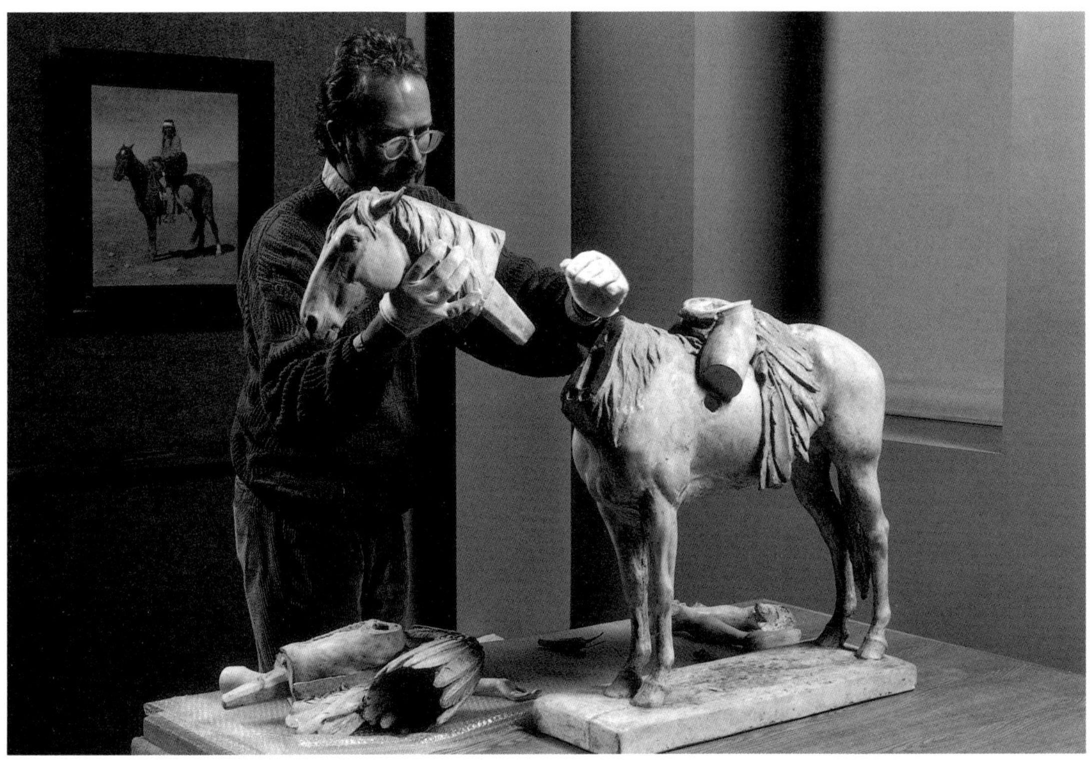

Fig. 17. Dallin's plaster *Appeal to the Great Spirit* being assembled at the Rockwell Museum in 1991.

bronze and the smaller version from the Department of State.

The *Appeal to the Great Spirit* was a favorite with educational institutions, and the image often became an important symbol in yearbooks and the like. At Central High in Tulsa, the thirty-six-inch bronze is meant to represent "...a symbol of the highest attainment of a worthy character."[91] Many schools that could not afford bronzes bought high quality plaster casts by P. P. Caproni and Brother instead. The agreement between Caproni and Dallin for the *Appeal to the Great Spirit* stipulated that he would receive a royalty for each plaster sold, plus one free cast.[92] Twenty-five of Dallin's sculptures were advertised in the 1915 catalogue *Caproni Casts, American Indians and Other Sculpture,* and in this manner the firm helped popularize his work.

The plaster version of the *Appeal to the Great Spirit* (No. 12) is strikingly similar in detail to the Dartmouth bronze and other known Gorham casts of this size. This plaster came to the Rockwell Museum in parts, and before it was assembled, the Roman joints typically employed by Caproni were clearly evident (see Fig. 17 and note 90). The excellence of the detail suggests that this may be an early Caproni cast that was poured but not assembled.

vii

Native American subjects remained an important part of Dallin's *oeuvre* throughout his career. While many were cast in bronze, others were cast only in plaster during his lifetime. East coast subjects also entered his work,

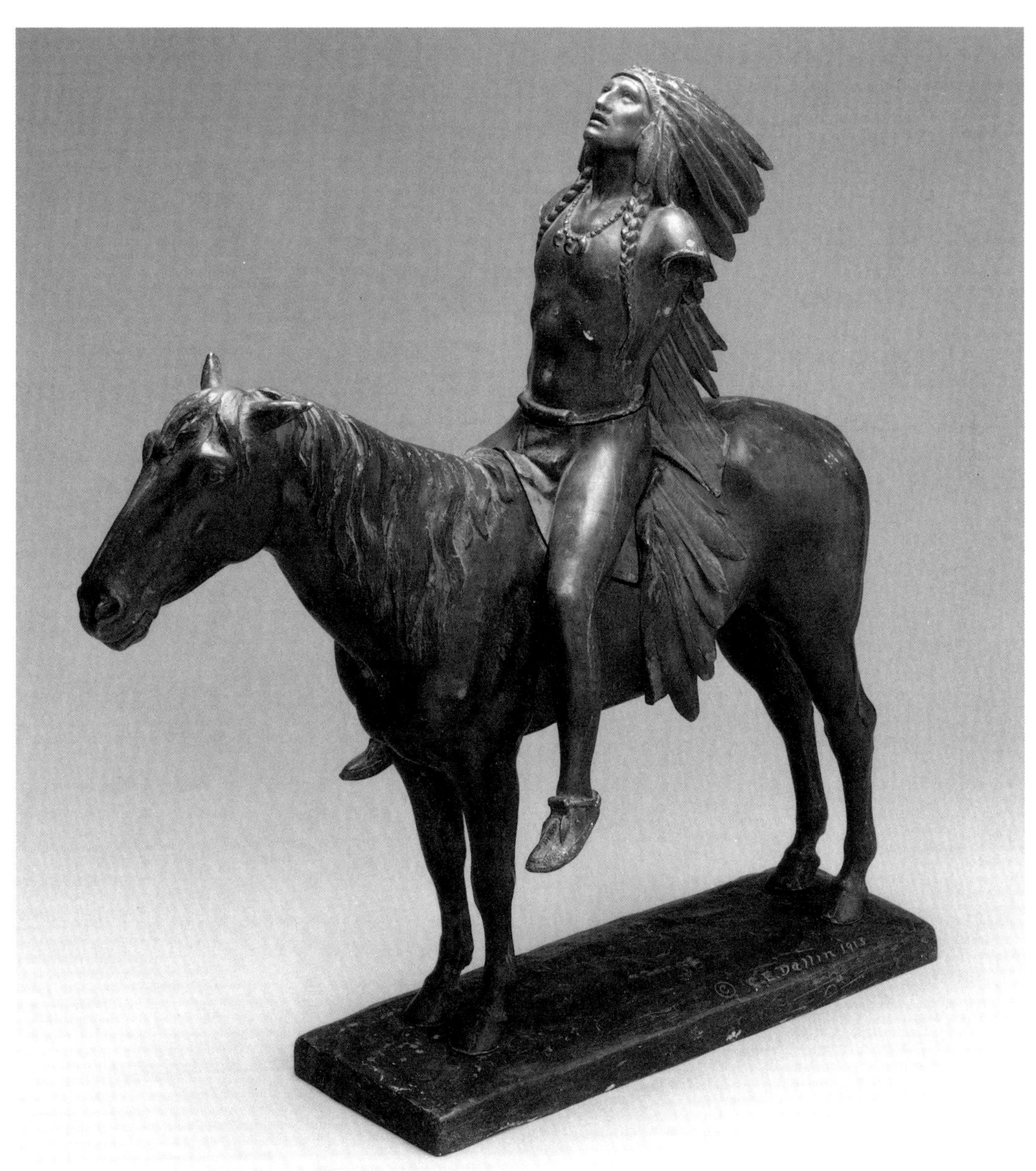

No. 45. Dallin. *Appeal to the Great Spirit.*

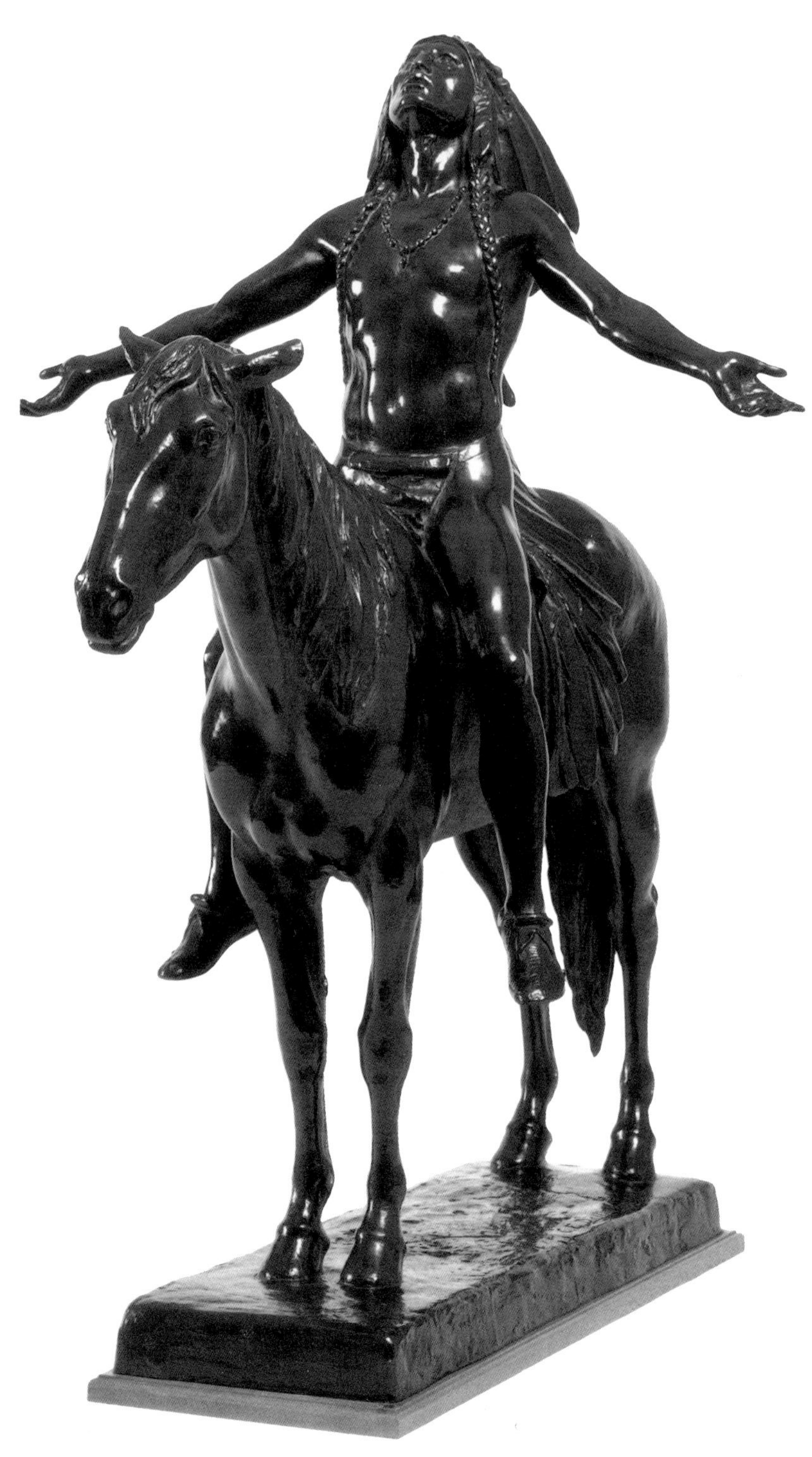

No. 11. Dallin. *Appeal to the Great Spirit*.

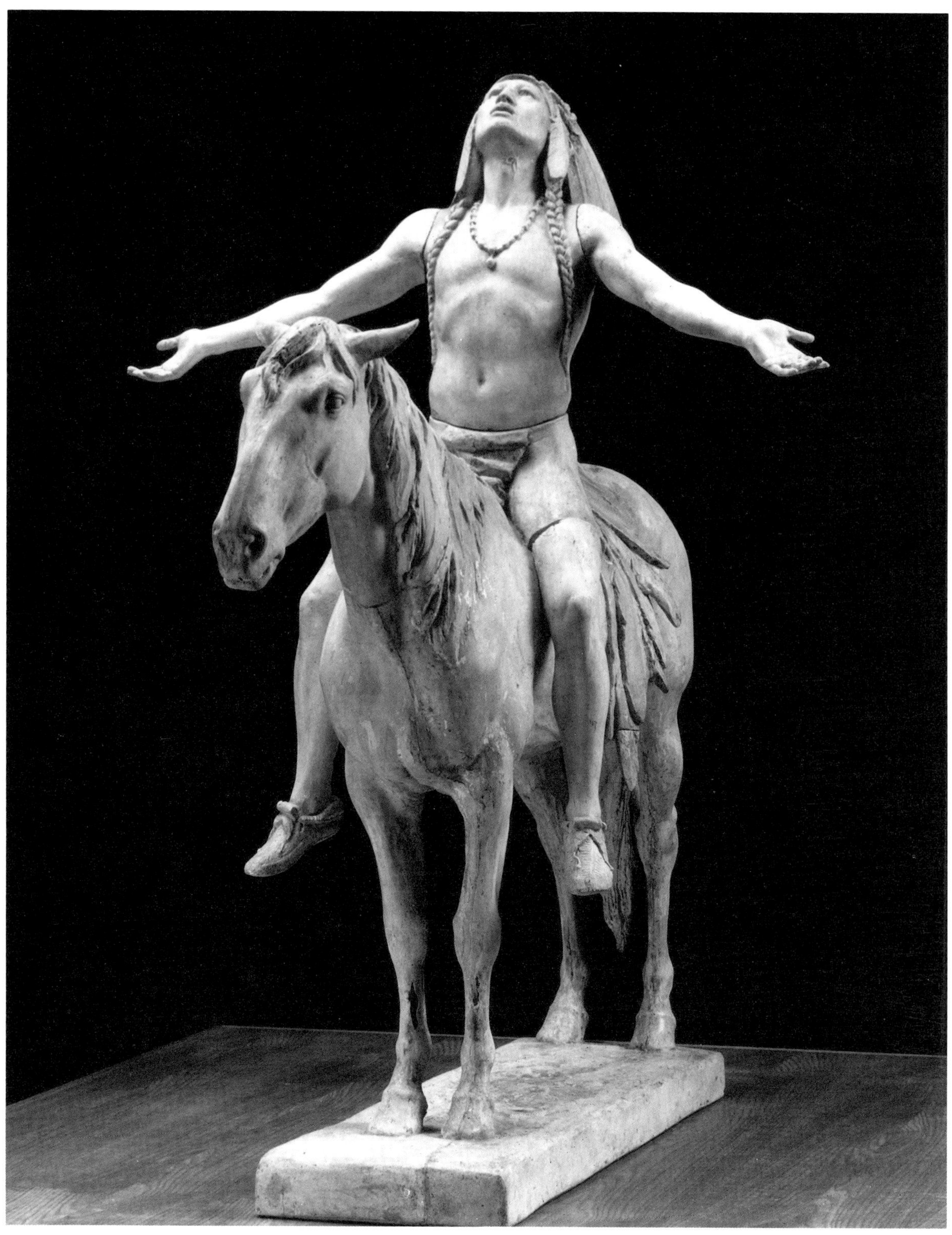

No. 12. Dallin. *Appeal to the Great Spirit* (before conservation).

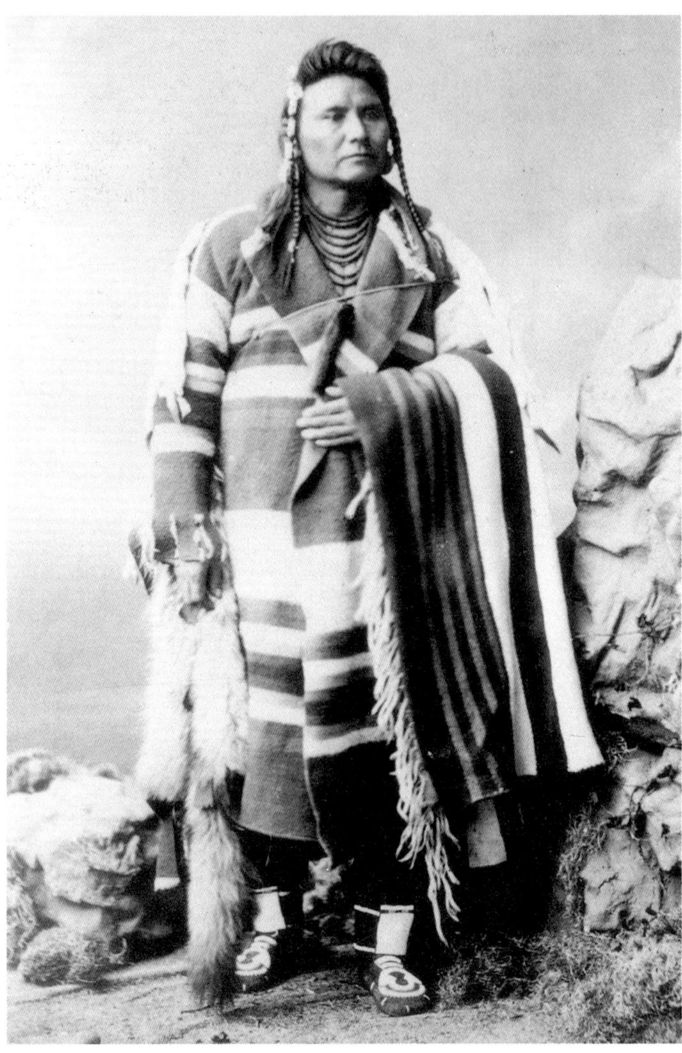

Fig. 18. Chief Joseph, Nez Perce. Buffalo Bill Historical Center, Cody, Wyoming. Vincent Mercaldo Collection.

either as commissions or on speculation.

Rell Francis writes that Dallin's original design for the *Appeal to the Great Spirit* may have also contained two standing figures, which were removed at the suggestion of Daniel Chester French.[93] The concept for two small bronzes—*War or Peace* and *Standing Figure of a Native American Chief (Chief Joseph)*—may date back to that design, or before.[94] Perhaps both are tributes to Chief Joseph, the great Nez Perce leader who died in 1904; after his people were forced to leave their ancestral lands, Chief Joseph sought to lead them to sanctuary in Canada, but was stopped by Colonel Nelson A. Miles in October 1877 in the Bear Paw Mountains. His statement of surrender to Miles, which is quoted here from the eyewitness account of Lieutenant Charles E. S. Wood, reflects his nobility: "'...I am tired of fighting. Our chiefs are killed.... It is cold, and we have no blankets. The little children are freezing to death. My people—some of them—have run away to the hills, and have no blankets, no food.... I want to have time to look for my children, and to see how many of them I can find; may be I shall find them among the dead. Hear me, my chiefs; my heart is sick and sad. From where the sun *now*

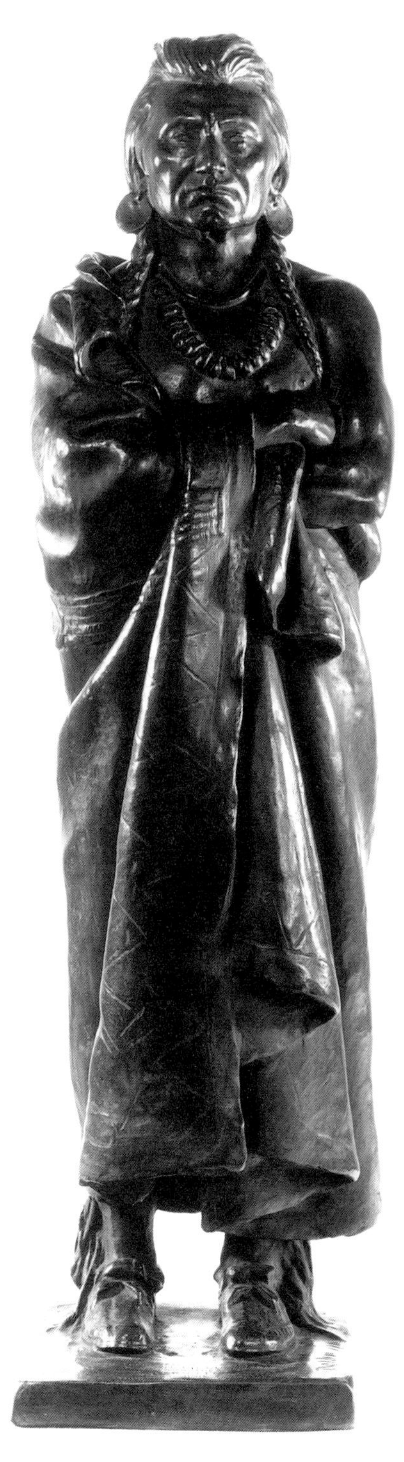

No. 18. Dallin. *Standing Figure of a Native American Chief (Chief Joseph)*. Collection of The New-York Historical Society.

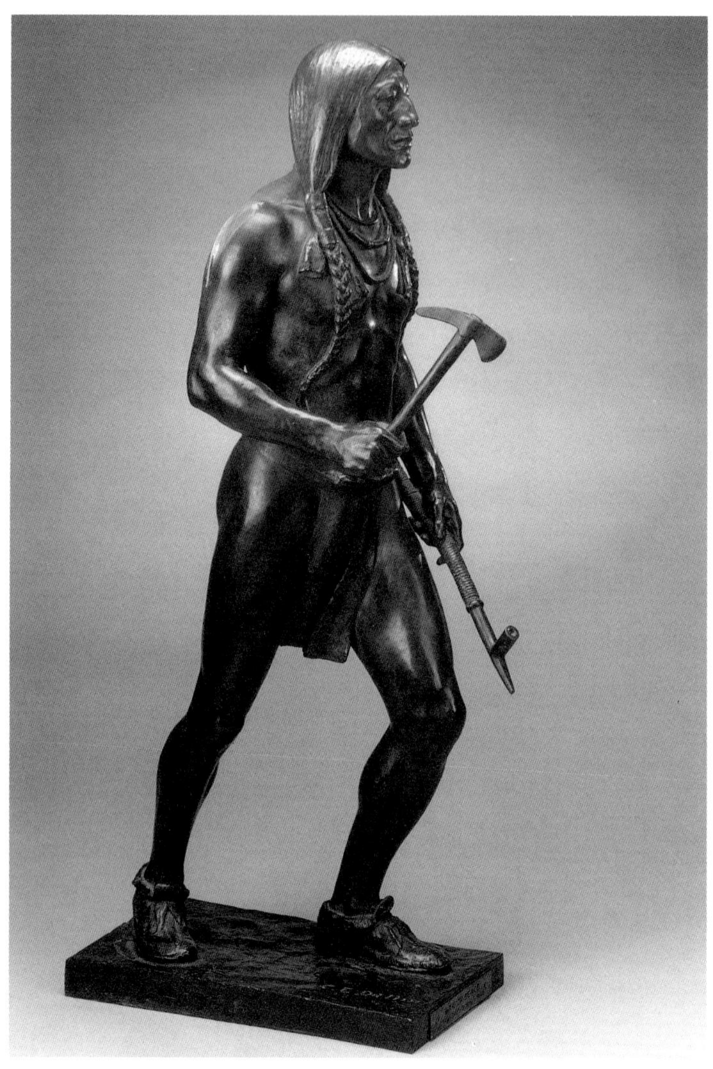

No. 17. Dallin.
War or Peace.

stands, I will fight no more forever!'"[95] Dallin's *Standing Figure of a Native American Chief* (No. 18) was modeled after one of the historical photographs of Chief Joseph (Fig. 18), but was probably inspired also by published accounts (one is reminded that when Chief Joseph surrendered, Dallin was a lad in Springville, and that shortly before Chief Joseph's death he had appeared at the Saint Louis Exposition, where Dallin's *Protest* was being exhibited). *War or Peace* (No. 17) is a more ambivalent subject: the figure strides forward forcefully, but not aggressively, the raised tomahawk suggesting the will to fight in defense of his people, the pipe suggesting the desire for peace. Dallin's powerful figure is broadly modeled, and the details of the accessories are restrained in a manner that favors compositional unity over picturesque detail. The rich dark patina is characteristic of the Roman Bronze Works.[96]

Dallin was fond of hunting and played baseball for the St. Botolph Club, but he excelled in archery. His *Archery Lesson* was offered as a

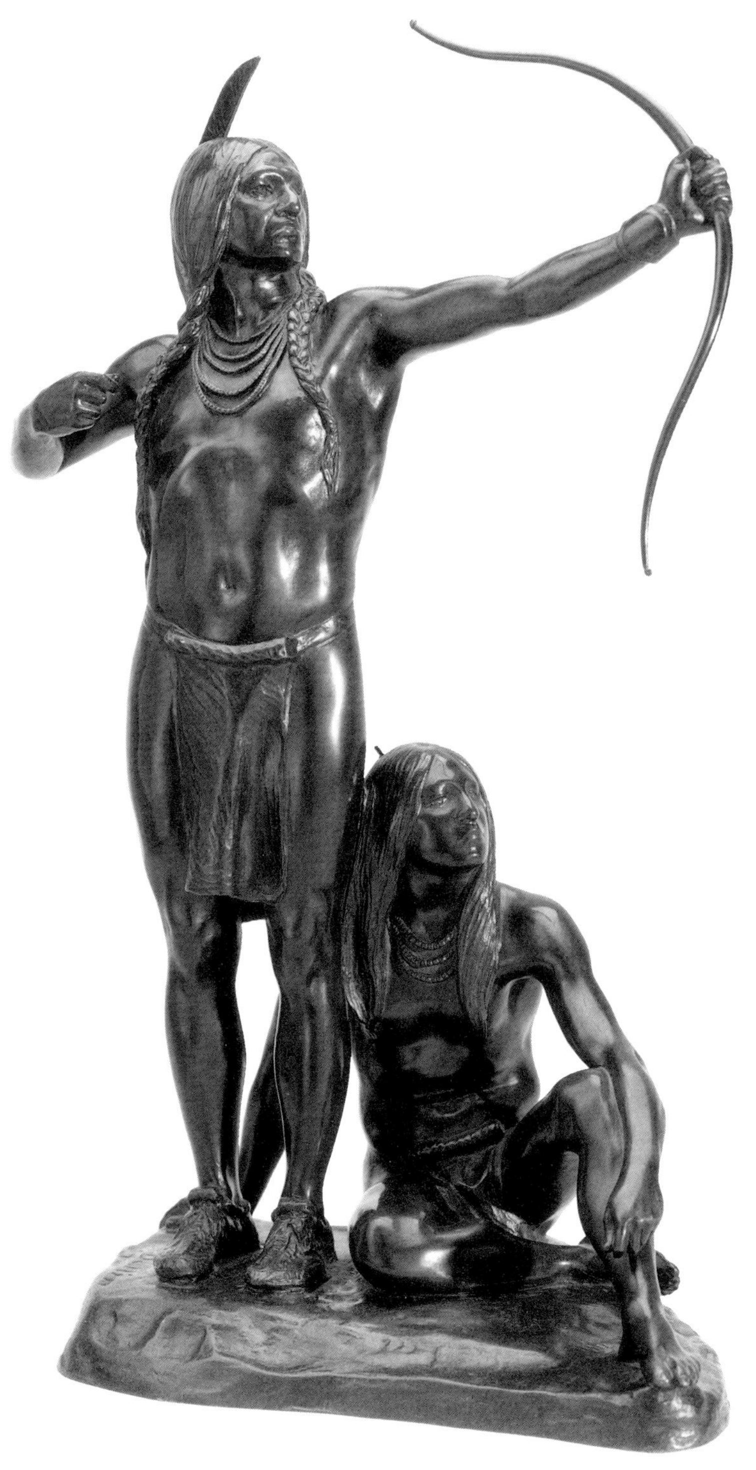

No. 19. Dallin. *Archery Lesson*.

trophy by the National Archery Association at the Chicago meeting in 1907. That particular statuette, which is known by old newspaper illustrations, seems to differ in detail from the bronze in this exhibition (No. 19).[97] Years earlier, Dallin had experimented with an archer motif in his lost *Indian Hunter* (1888), which won a medal in New York.[98] The archer is a subject that dates back to antiquity, one of the finest surviving examples being *Herakles,* from the Temple of Aegina (c. 490 B.C.). Germany saw in the 19th century a renewed interest in Greek art led by such artists as Adolph Hildebrand and his followers—including Tuaillon (Fig. 11). Dallin may have known Hildebrand's *Archery Lesson* (1888), a relief depicting an older man teaching a youth to shoot. He certainly would have been familiar with Saint-Gaudens's *Diana* (1891), which was intended for Madison Square Garden. His most immediate source of inspiration, however, was probably Hermon A. MacNeil's *Sun Vow* (1898), which represents a Native American initiation into manhood (Dallin and MacNeil had studied together with Chapu). Unlike MacNeil, whose brilliantly modeled figures and impressionistic detail activate the bronze surfaces, Dallin retained more sharply defined forms and crisp detail.

Surviving among the Caproni casts at Giust Gallery, Boston, is Dallin's *Indian Archer* (No. 22).[99] The handsomely modeled figure stands firmly with both feet planted on the ground, his head turned slightly upward as he follows the flight of the arrow he has just discharged. There is a sense of total concentration that moves the work from the narrative to the symbolic. Dallin sculpted a number of archery

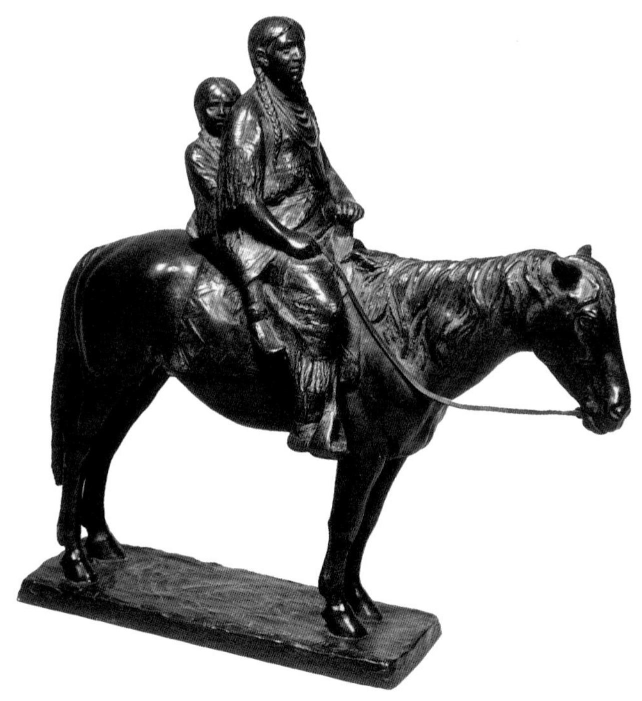

No. 16. Dallin. *Indian Squaw and Child on Horseback.*

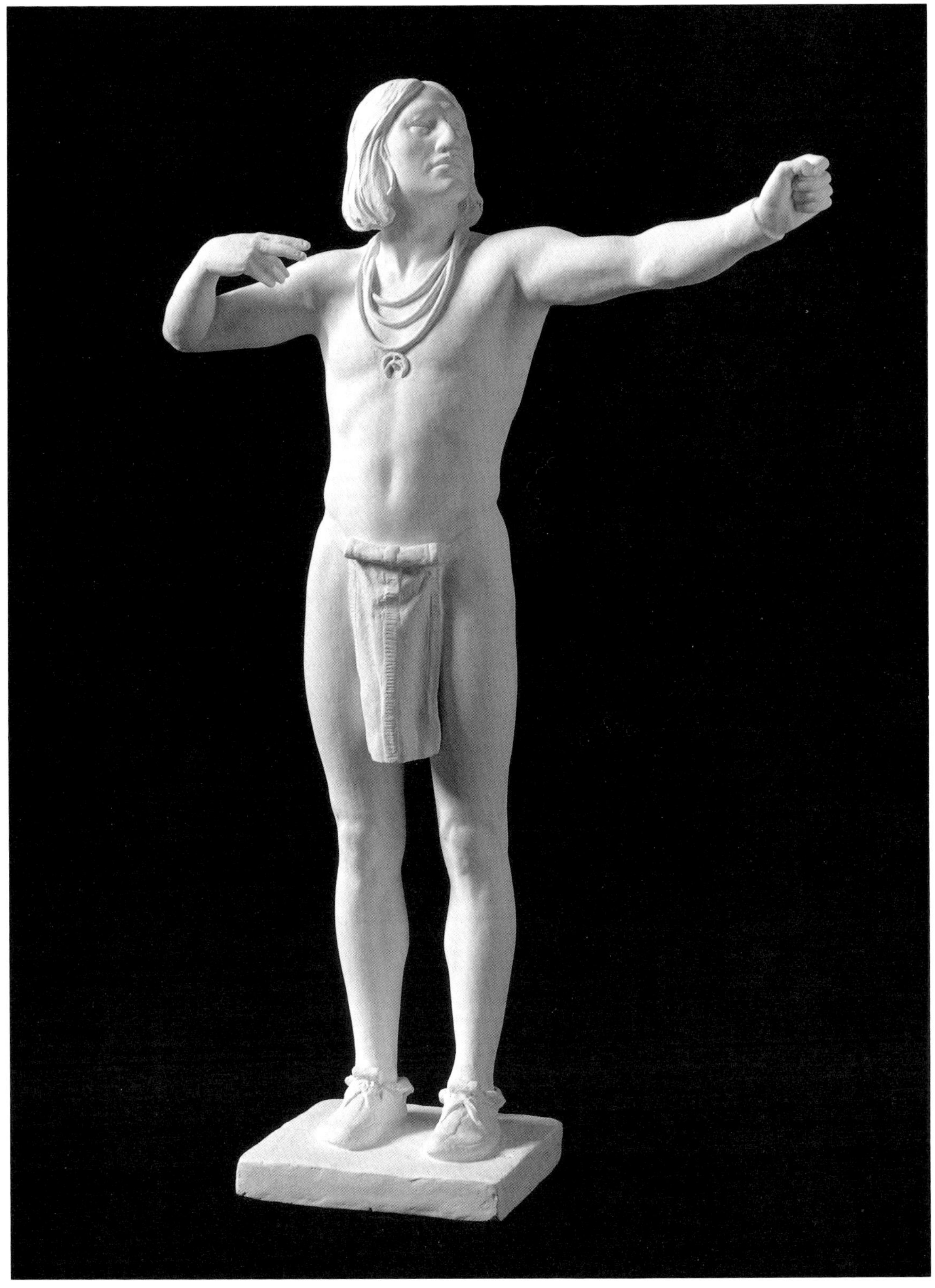

No. 22. Dallin. *Indian Archer*.

award medals, all incorporating the Native American, but only rarely did he represent a bowman discharging an arrow (No. 25).

When the new Arlington, Massachusetts, town hall was dedicated in 1913, two of Dallin's sculptures that were placed nearby were also unveiled—*Robbins Memorial Flagstaff* and *Menotomy Indian Hunter.*[100] Although the subject of the *Indian Hunter* was inspired in part by Judges VII: 4-7, Dallin said that the bronze was intended to represent a moment of pause to drink, "...with every line conveying the sense of poise and readiness to be off on the instant."[101] Dallin returned to the subject for his small statue *Indian Drinking* (No. 20) and for an *Eastern Archery Association* medal (No. 24).[102] The Atlanta bronze is probably the subject titled *Indian Hunter* that was exhibited at the St. Botolph Club in 1914 and at the Panama-Pacific Exposition the following year.[103] It is one of Dallin's most beautifully conceived and executed bronzes, and is distinguished by the broad modeling of the anatomy, while the braids falling gently down across the figure heighten the sensuous appeal of contrasting textures. Since the face is cast downward, it is not readily visible but possessed of a haunting quality characteristic of the period.

In addition to the *Pilgrim Half-Dollar,* discussed below, Dallin executed a number of important sculptures commemorating the three-hundredth anniversary of the Pilgrims' landing, among them *Massasoit,* chief of the Wampanoags who befriended the Pilgrims. The over life-size statue, which had been commissioned by the Improved Order of Red Men, was erected on Cole's Hill, Plymouth, Massachusetts, in 1921.[104] The design, however, originated some years earlier. Dallin's first small version of the subject, which was cast in plaster and bronze, was advertised in the Caproni catalogue (1915), but Dallin then revised the statue for Cole's Hill. In making his revisions, Dallin altered many of the inaccurate details of the first version.[105] Probably Dallin reworked the same design for *Massasoit* and for another statue titled *The Marksman* (No. 21); although they vary in detail, the poses are strikingly similar. *The Marksman* was awarded as the first prize trophy for the eighth annual shoot of the New England Rifle Association in 1912.[106]

* * * * *

One of Dallin's friends and private patrons was Geraldine Rockefeller Dodge, whose estate sale in 1975 included eighteen of his bronzes.[107] Two of these bronzes, which vary significantly in size and appearance, depict Native Americans standing with their left feet resting on buffalo skulls. Both deal with the subject of the last arrow, or the passing of the buffalo: Dallin caused some confusion by referring to the larger of the two by more than one title.[108] The over life-size statue, which is now in Muncie, was titled *The Passing of the Buffalo* in the Dodge sale; this bronze or an unlocated version of the subject was in the 1923 exhibition of the National Sculpture Society under the title *The Last Arrow.*[109] (Since the arrow that the statue held in 1923 was removed at some time, the title change may have represented for Dallin a more symbolic interpretation.) The smaller version of the subject (No. 23), which possesses an extremely fine patina, was cast in Munich and bears a copyright date of 1926. This is probably the bronze titled *The Last Arrow* that was exhibited at Grand Central Galleries in 1927.[110]

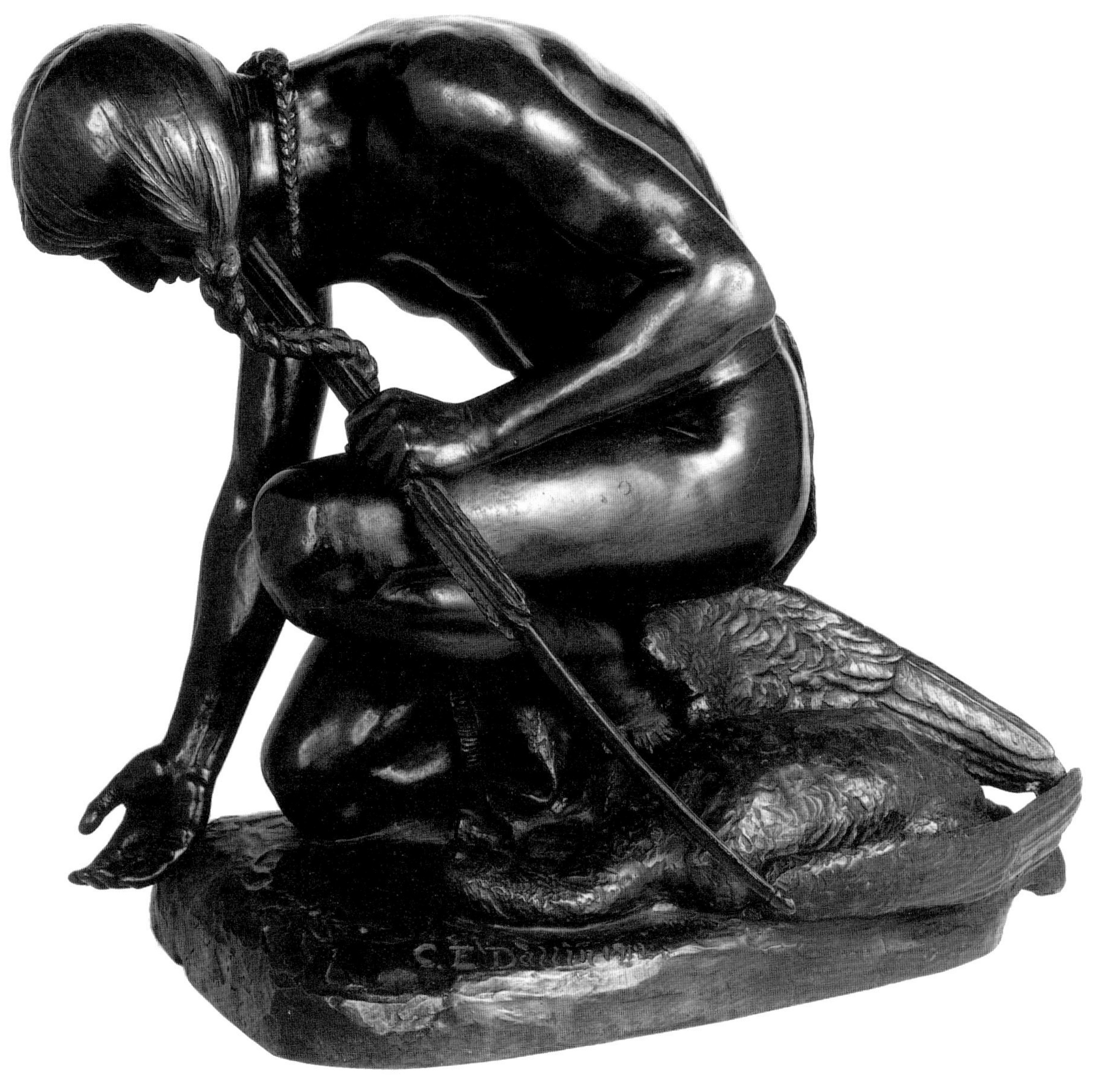

No. 20. Dallin. *Indian Drinking.*

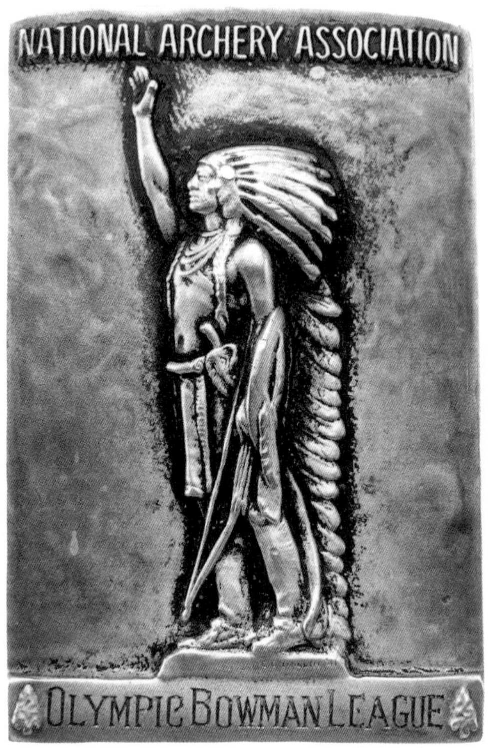

No. 26. Dallin. *National Archery Association*.

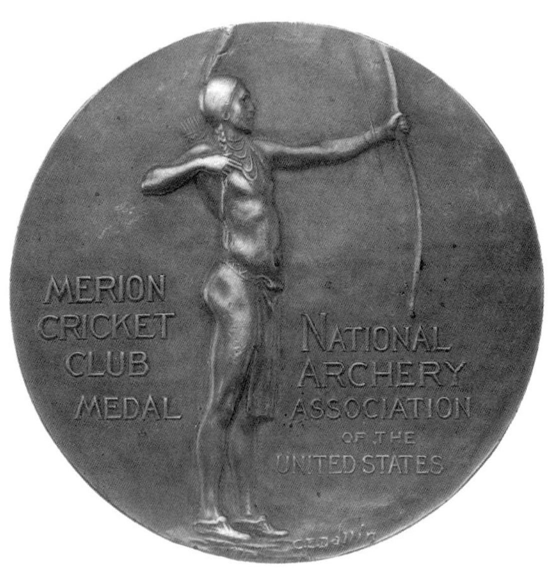

No. 25. Dallin. *Merion Cricket Club Medal*.

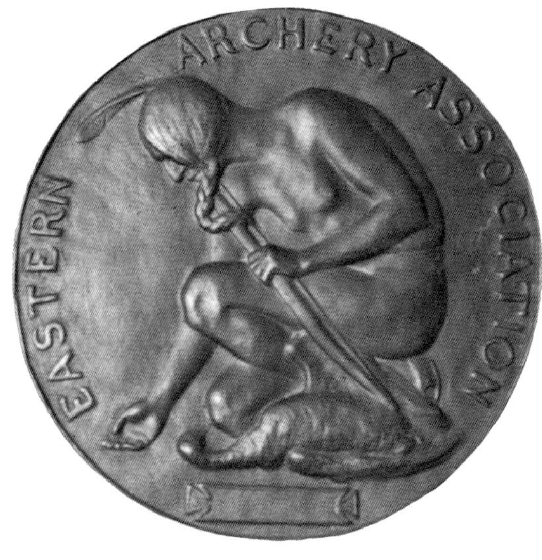

No. 24. Dallin. *Eastern Archery Association*.

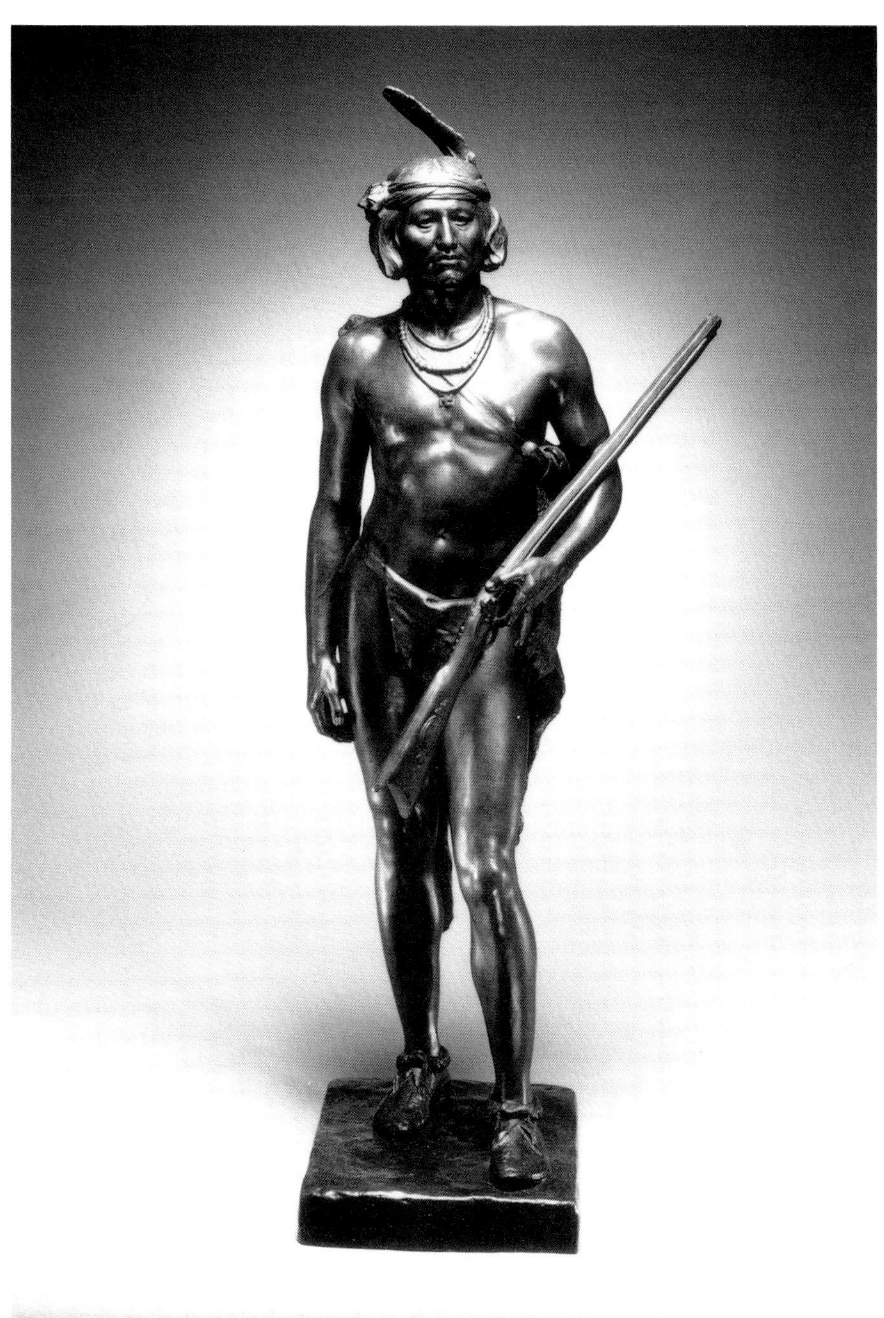

No. 21. Dallin. *The Marksman*. © 1993 Sotheby's, Inc.

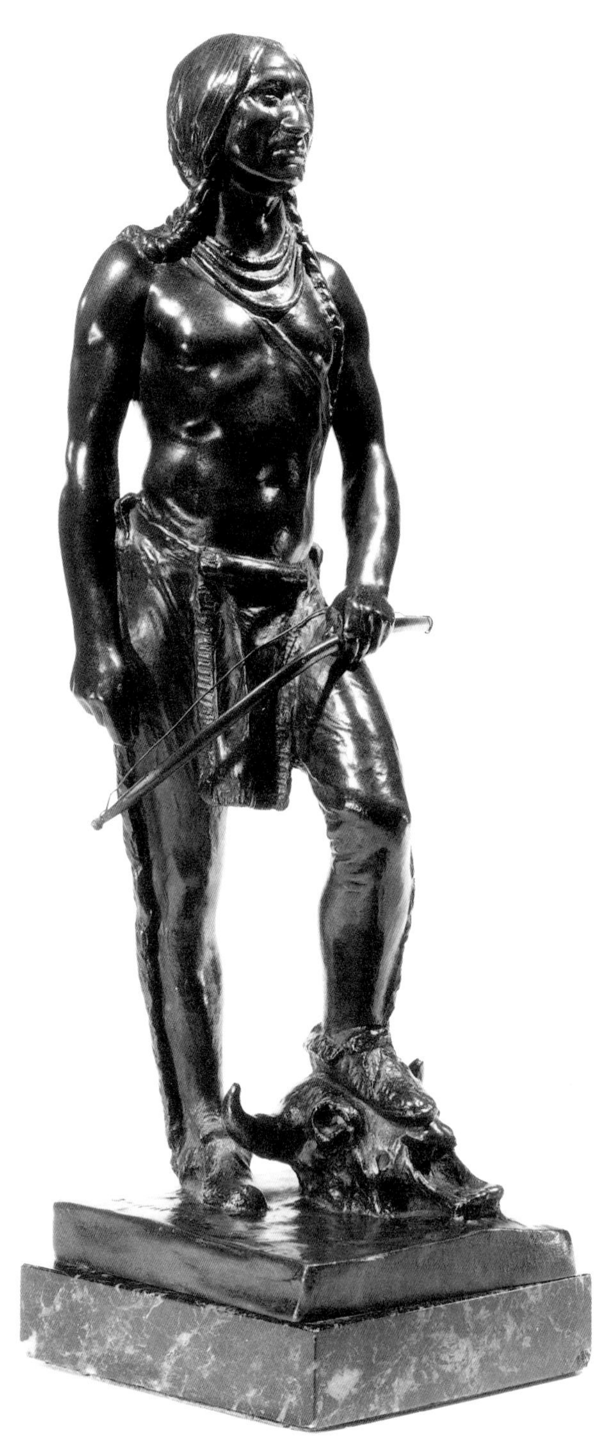

No. 23. Dallin. *The Last Arrow*.

For Native Americans, the buffalo skull symbolized the power of natural spirits, and it became a center for ceremonial ritual. Edward Sheriff Curtis recorded such ceremonies in photographs like *Prayer to the Mystery*. Frederic Remington painted *Conjuring Back the Buffalo* (c. 1892), N. C. Wyeth *Invocation for the Buffalo* (c. 1900) and Joseph Henry Sharp *Prayer to the Spirit of the Buffalo* (1910); each reveals a variety of artistic conventions. In the small *Last Arrow,* Dallin advanced his artistic license, for the buffalo skull was sacred and would not have been stepped upon, especially in a ceremonial context. But the artist was unable to escape the influence of European sculptural tradition, especially Donatello's *David* (1430s), where the youth's left foot rests lightly upon the severed head of Goliath (the Dallins had made a trip to Italy in 1924-25). That artists in their depicting the American West remained under the influence of European artistic tradition is seen to further

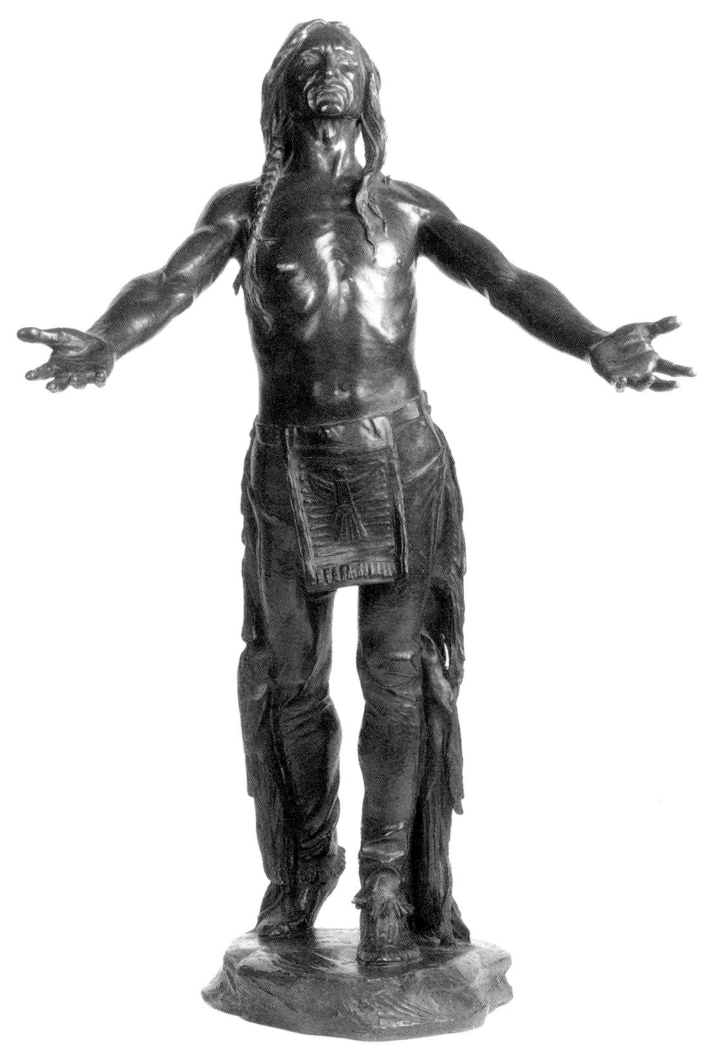

Fig. 19. Charles H. Humphriss. *Appeal to the Great Spirit*. 1906.
From the Collection of Gilcrease Museum, Tulsa.

advantage by comparing the subject of the *Appeal to the Great Spirit* by Dallin with that of Charles H. Humphriss (Fig. 19): the motif of the outstretched arms of the supplicants has a long history in European art, for example, the passion of Christ or Saint Francis receiving the stigmata.

In a 1925 interview, Dallin discussed his dream for a memorial to the Native Americans, which he hoped would be in Washington, and he was working at that time on several large heads: "'I like to work on four or five heads at the same time.... While working on one head I get an idea I can use on another....'" The project was not realized, however, and the heads are now scattered.[111]

viii

Besides his work depicting Native Americans, between 1900 and his death in 1944, Dallin executed a broad range of ideal subjects in a manner consistent with the continuing academic tradition, and the influence of other artists trained in France is especially evident. His reputation was bolstered by the prizes he won at the various Expositions, the exhibition of his work in Boston and New York, and by his successful competition for the large Civil War memorial in Syracuse. He was the recipient of public and private commissions. And he turned his attention to a variety of academic subjects—portrait reliefs and medals, war memorials, symbolic figures, portraiture and American history, to summarize broadly. Unfortunately, Dallin left few sketches and models; his working method was to develop his ideas in clay, and he probably destroyed many unsuccessful designs in order to reuse the materials.[112]

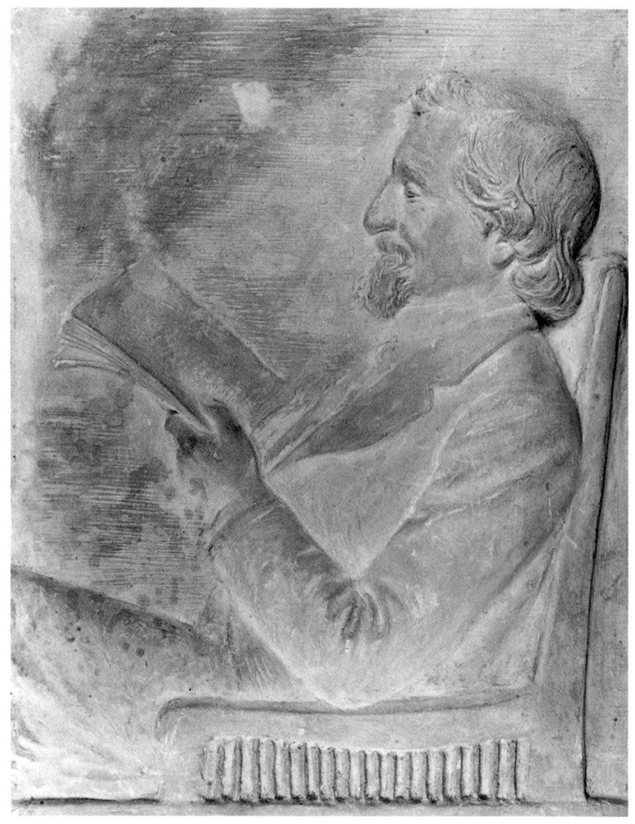

No. 27. Dallin. *John Townsend Trowbridge*.

Dallin made about forty-five relief panels during his career, especially in his later years.[113] A selection of these permit, in the format of an exhibition, a view of Dallin's ideal subjects. *John Townsend Trowbridge* (Nos. 27 and 28) reflects Dallin's interest in the Beaux-Arts revival of Renaissance relief portraiture. Dallin made two copies of the *Trowbridge* bronze for the subject's grandchildren. Since Trowbridge lived in Arlington, these reliefs were probably a private commission between colleagues—the popular 19th-century author and the sculptor. Trowbridge, who was born in Ogden, New York, in 1827, was one of the original contributors to *The Atlantic Monthly* with his entry "Pendlam; A Modern Reformer," and he counted among his friends Walt Whitman, Ralph

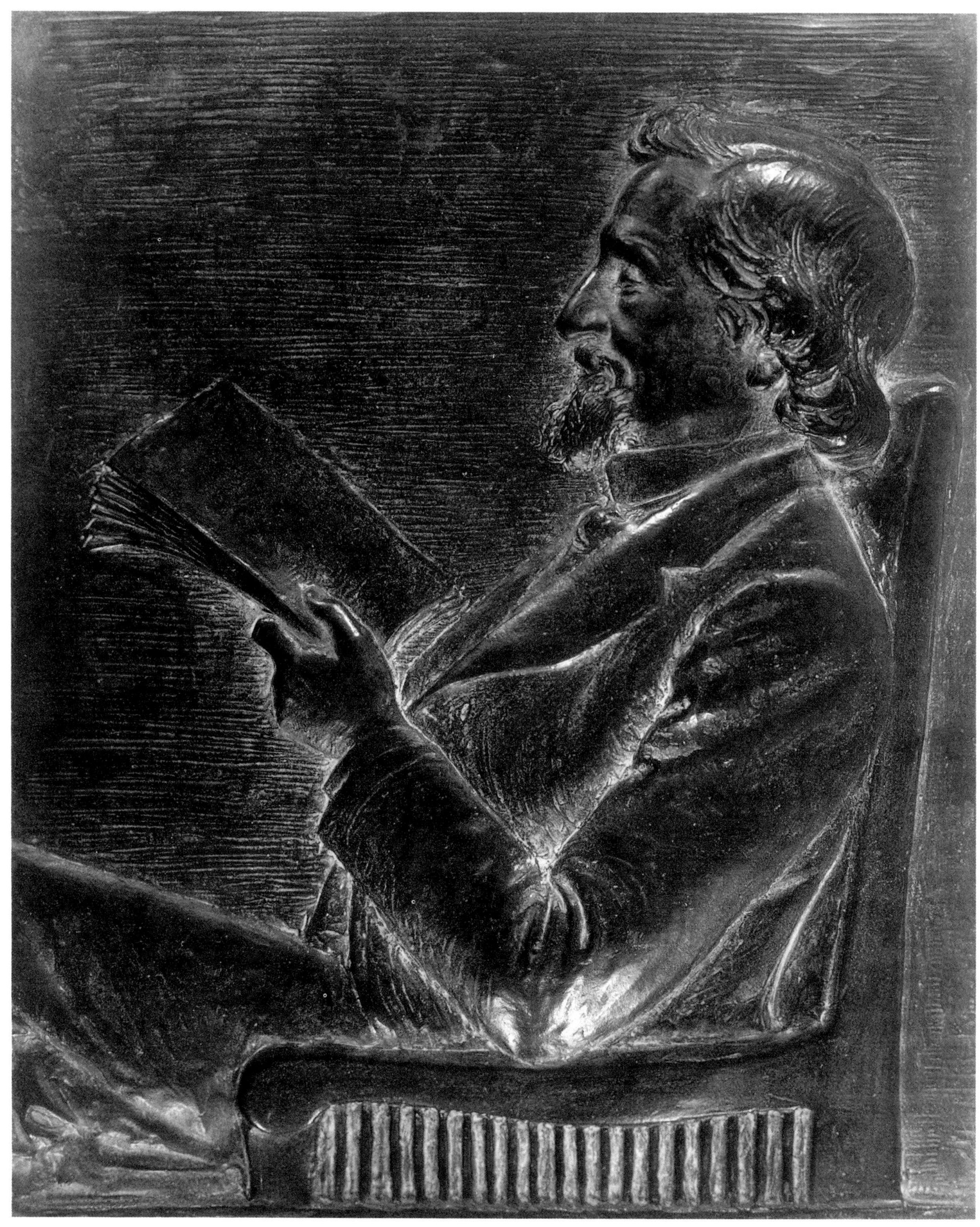

No. 28. Dallin. *John Townsend Trowbridge*.

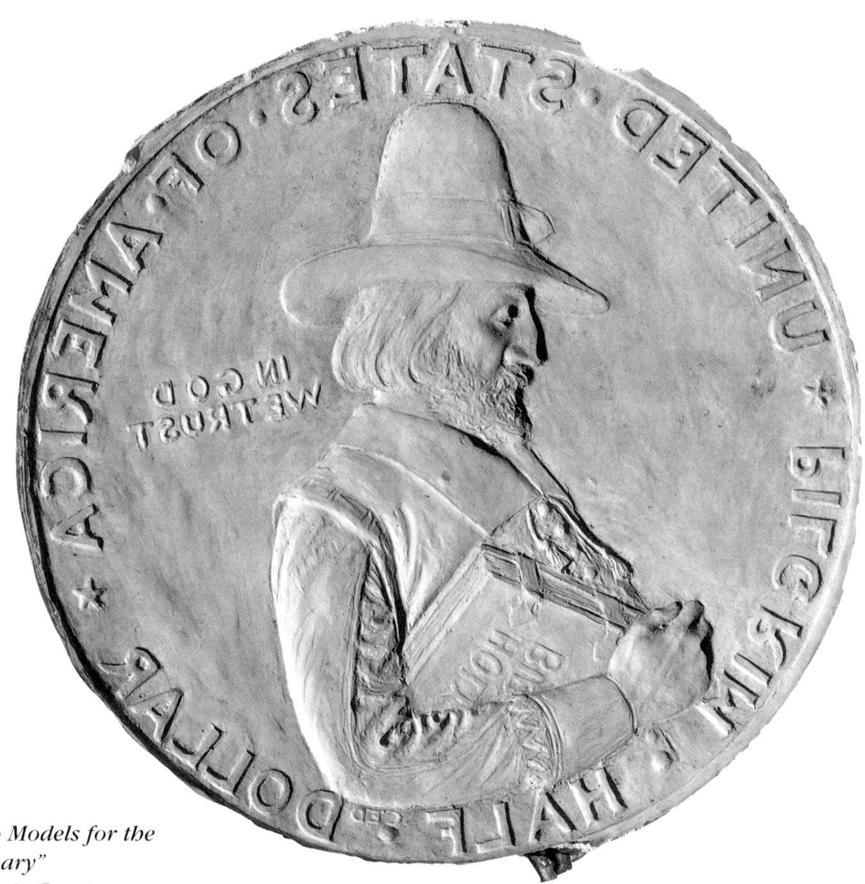

No. 30. Dallin. *Two Models for the "Pilgrim Tercentenary" Half-Dollar* (obverse). Courtesy Museum of Fine Arts, Boston.

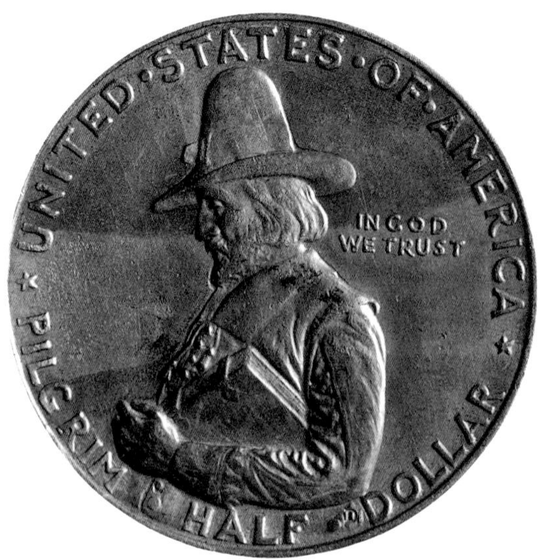

No. 29. Dallin. *Pilgrim Half-Dollar* (obverse).

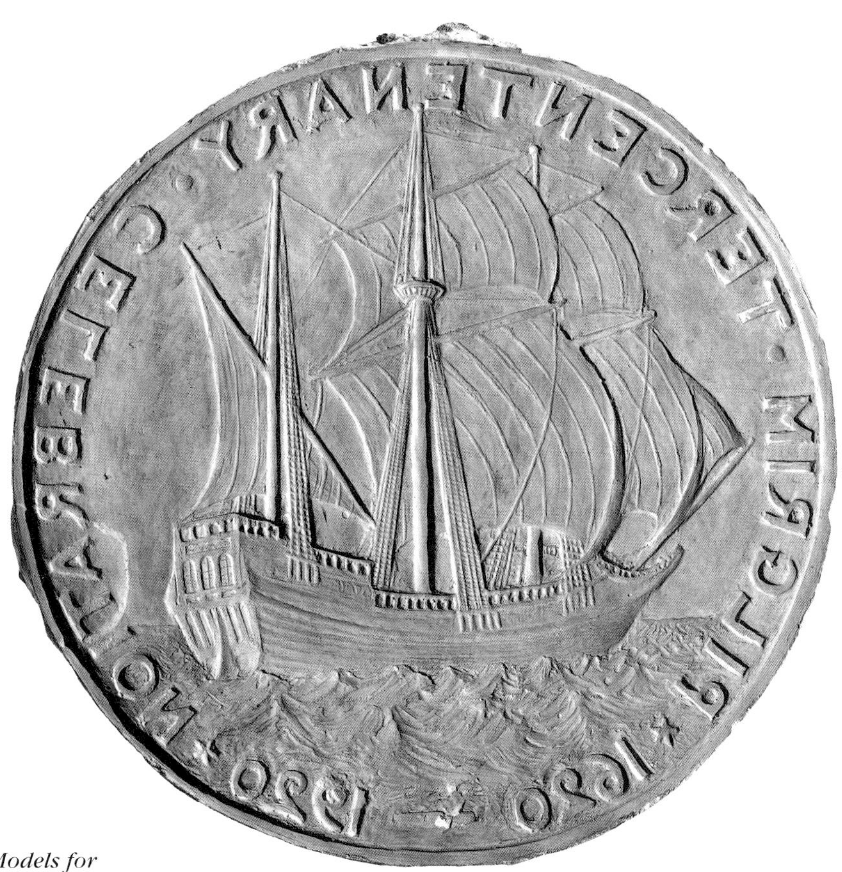

No. 30. Dallin. *Two Models for the "Pilgrim Tercentenary" Half-Dollar* (reverse). Courtesy Museum of Fine Arts, Boston.

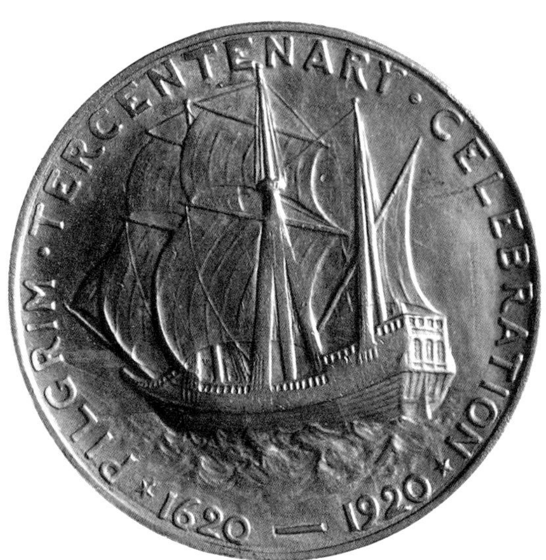

No. 29. Dallin. *Pilgrim Half-Dollar* (reverse).

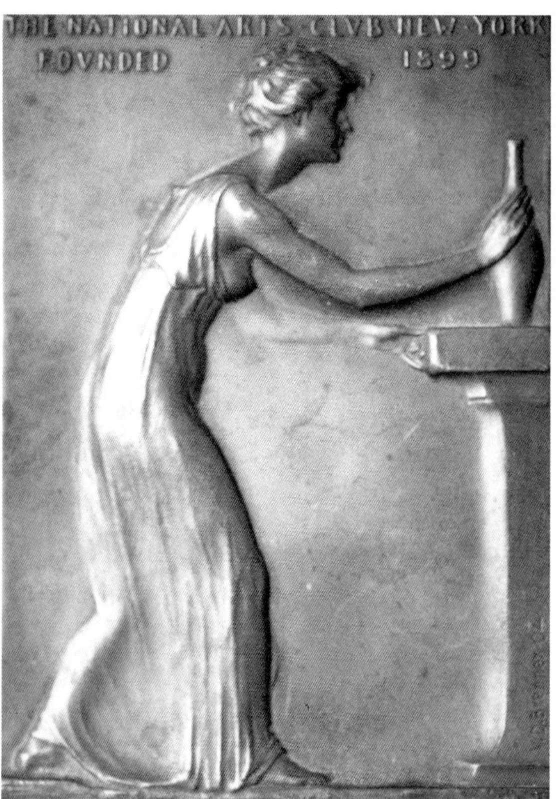

No. 32. Dallin. *The National Arts Club, New York.*

Waldo Emerson and Henry Wadsworth Longfellow. His first book, *Father Brighthopes* (1853), was followed by a long list of novels and poems that have since fallen into obscurity.[114]

Dallin's *Pilgrim Half-Dollar*, which is exhibited along with the large plaster models (Nos. 29 and 30), has been called "...a masterpiece in the conservative tradition," by Cornelius Vermeule, who also points out the innovative nature of the slightly rough background surfaces to suggest modeling. The influence of Saint-Gaudens is seen in the coin's high edge and the figure of William Bradford, which recalls *The Puritan* (1886).[115] Mrs. Dallin wrote that in 1921 Dallin's medal honoring Marshal Ferdinand Foch (No. 31) was presented to the celebrated World War I Commander-In-Chief of the Allies at the Boston State House. Vermeule refers to the *Foch* medal as an "...effort in conventional classicism."[116] A more simplified design is seen in his *National Arts Club* medal (No. 32), in which a classically inspired female figure is placed against an undefined background. He designed the *Massachusetts Normal Art School Medal of Honor* (No. 33) to commemorate the fiftieth anniversary of the school's founding (the reverse was designed by Raymond Porter).[117] The *Beverly Hospital* medal (No. 34) and the *Theodore William Richards* medal (No. 35), which was awarded for excellence in chemistry, date from 1930; Richards, who was a professor at Harvard University, was the son of the landscape painter William Trost Richards.[118]

* * * * *

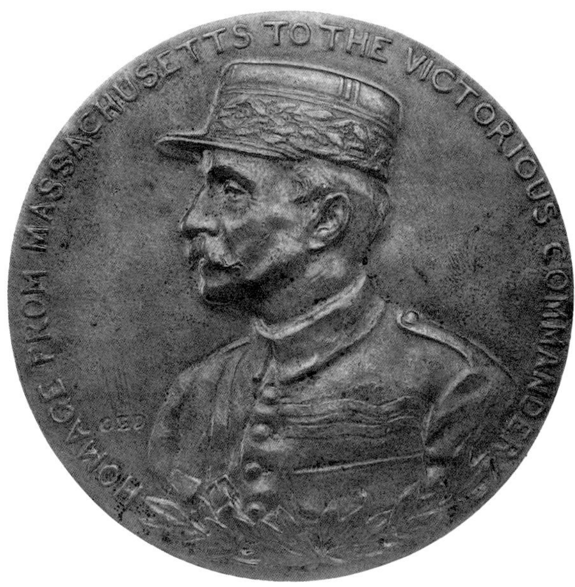

No. 31. Dallin. *Homage from Massachusetts to the Victorious Commander* (obverse).

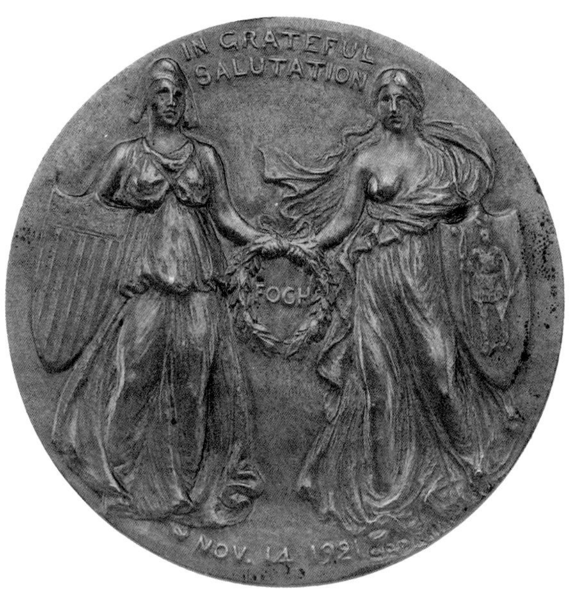

No. 31. Dallin. *Homage from Massachusetts to the Victorious Commander* (reverse).

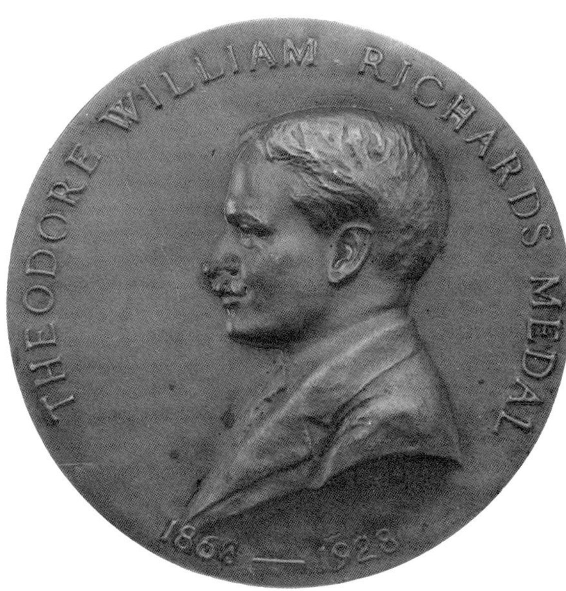

No. 35. Dallin. *Theodore William Richards Medal* (obverse).

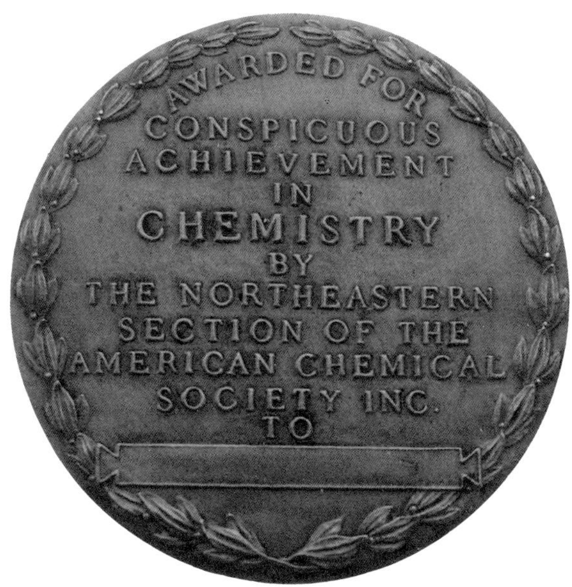

No. 35. Dallin. *Theodore William Richards Medal* (reverse).

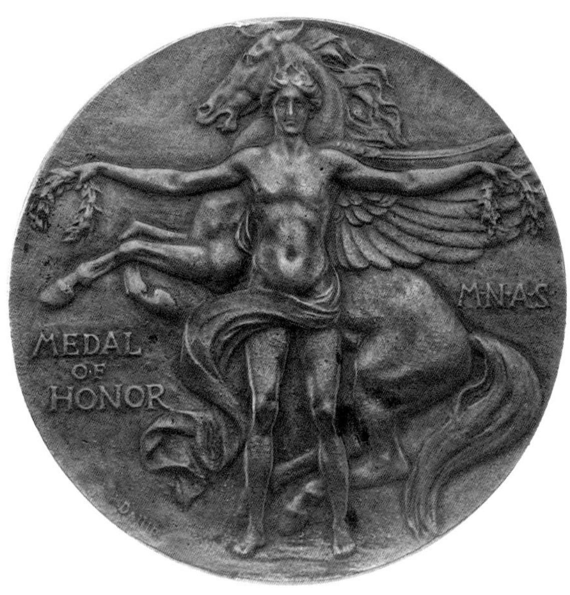

No. 33. Dallin. *Medal of Honor, Massachusetts Normal Art School.*

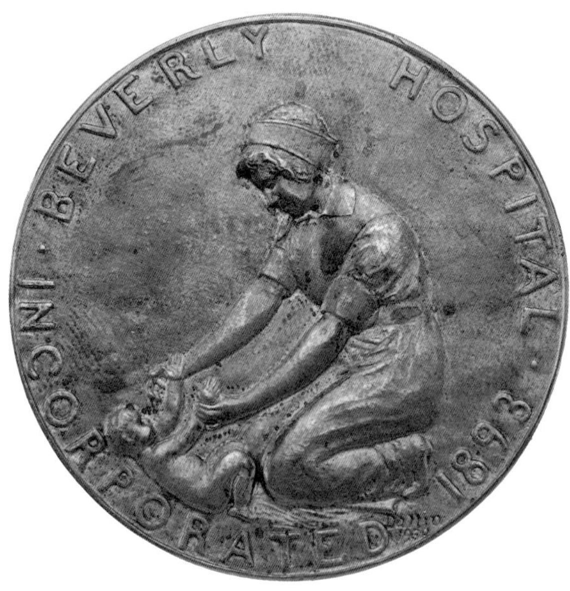

No. 34. Dallin. *Beverly Hospital Incorporated.*

The Civil War created a national demand for public monuments commemorating historic battles and fallen heroes that reached a crescendo in the late 19th century and spilled over into the 20th. Unfortunately, no models or sketches by Dallin in this genre are known to exist, although these monuments are an essential aspect of his career. Dallin's panel depicting the departing troops on the Woburn Memorial (1904), which was a collaboration between the sculptor and the architect J. M. Portal, was inspired by Saint-Gaudens's great Memorial to Robert Gould Shaw (1897), without the latter's vigor.[119] The cavalry skirmish fought in Hanover, June 30, 1863, was commemorated by Dallin's *The Picket* (1905) (Fig. 20). A reporter's remark is revealing: "...The quiet horse with the rider [the picket] ready for instant movement...appealed to his [Dallin's] imagination more than if the animal were in more violent action...."[120] The following year (1906) Dallin won a competition for the Soldiers' and Sailors' Monument in Syracuse; the jury included John Q. A. Ward and French.[121] To architect Clarence Blackall's stone pylon are attached Dallin's two deep bronze reliefs—the less successful *Incident at Gettysburg* and the *Call to Arms,* which is reminiscent of Rude's *The Marseillaise.* In 1908 Dallin returned to Paris with his family to prepare the *Appeal to the Great Spirit* and the Syracuse reliefs for casting.[122] Some years later Dallin sculpted *General Winfield S. Hancock* (1913) for the Pennsylvania Memorial at Gettysburg.[123]

* * * * *

The World Wars touched Dallin deeply. His son Arthur won the Croix de Guerre for bravery as an ambulance driver during World War I and then lost his life in action at the beginning

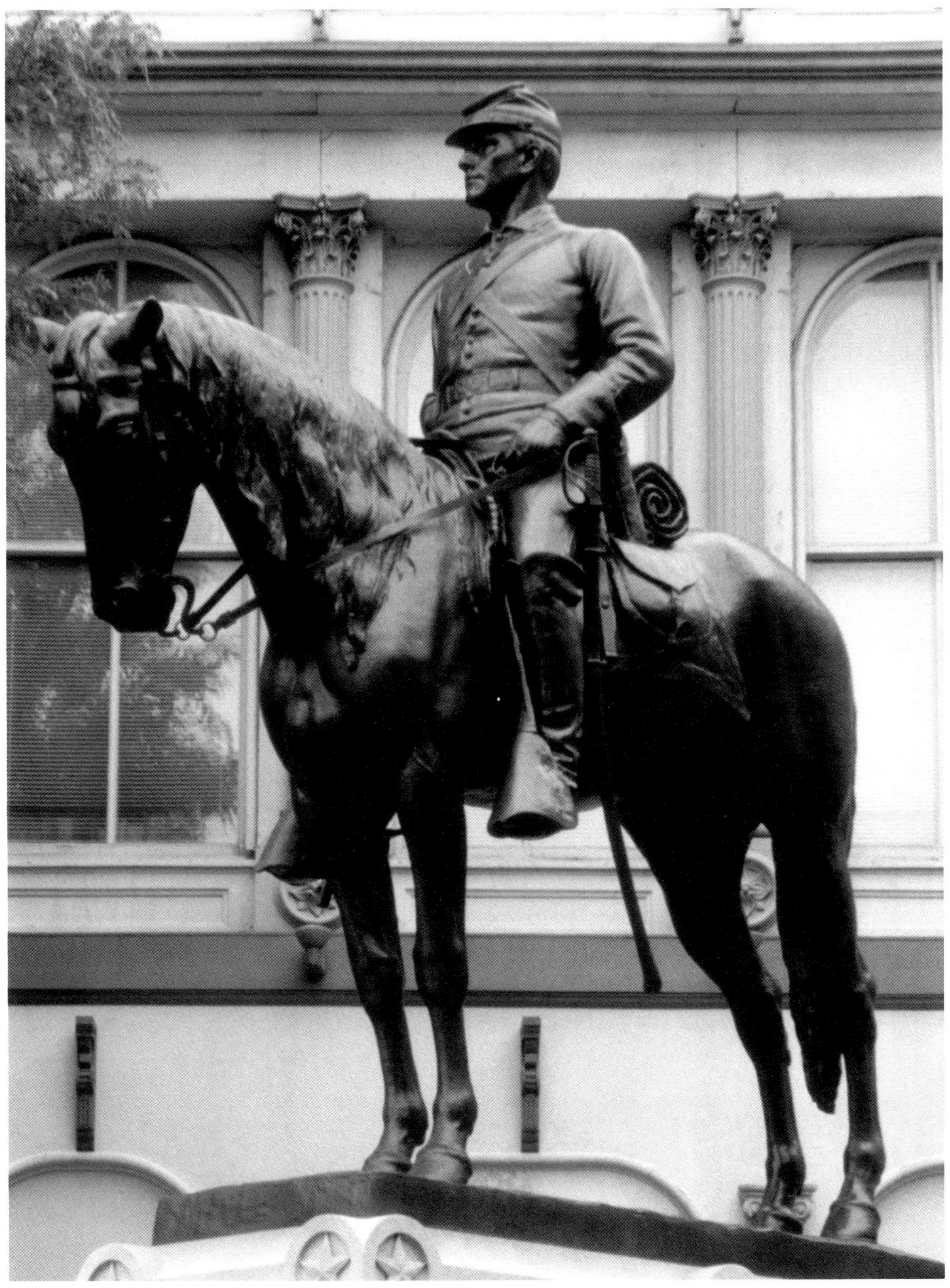

Fig. 20. Dallin. *The Picket*. 1904. Hanover, Pennsylvania.

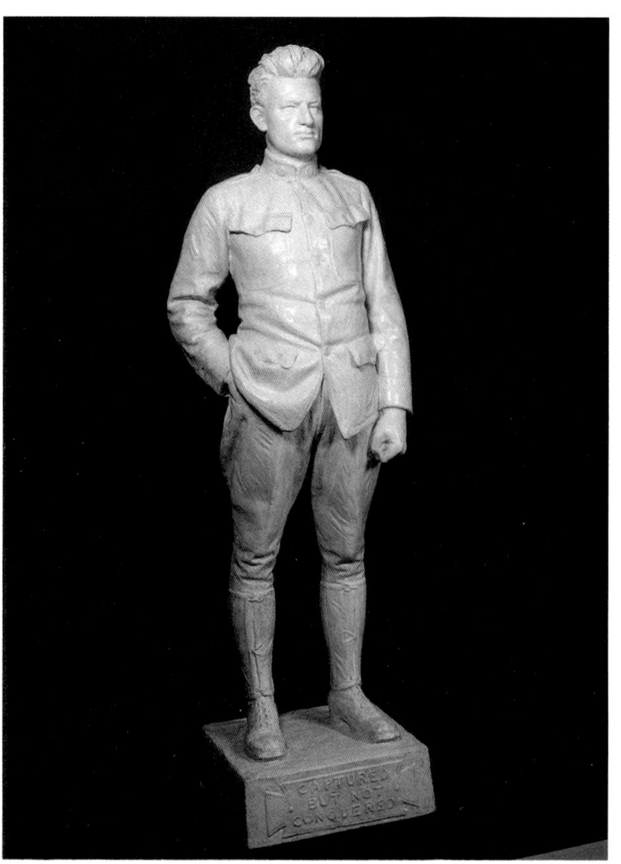

No. 36. Dallin. *Captured But Not Conquered.*

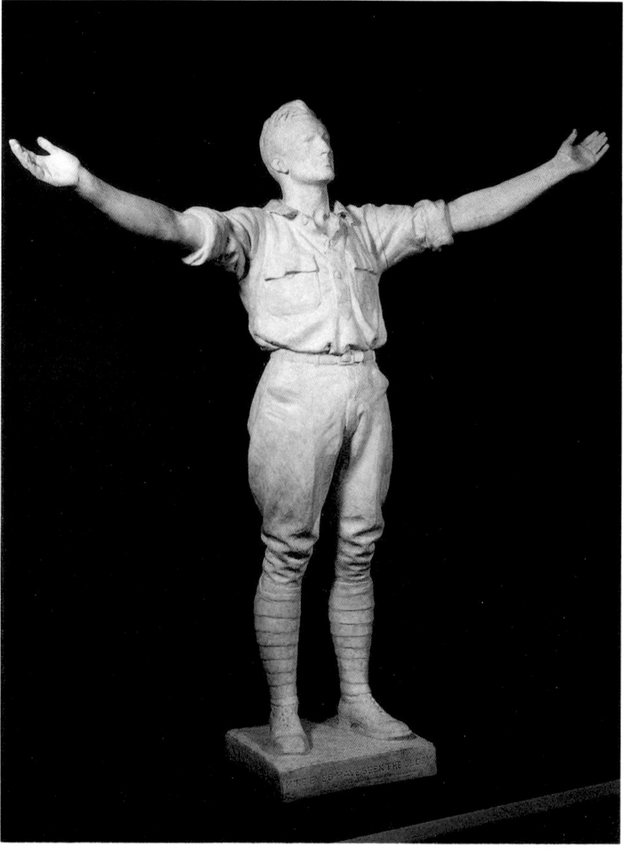
No. 38. Dallin. *Mine Eyes Have Seen The Glory.*

of World War II. The whereabouts of Dallin's plaster statuette of Arthur in an ambulance uniform (c. 1917-18) is unknown, but two other doughboy subjects survive.[124] *Captured But Not Conquered* was inspired by a photograph of Sergeant Edgar M. Halyburton that was originally published by the German press, then picked up by the American press.[125] The statue of Halyburton, who was reportedly the first American prisoner taken, was Dallin's contribution to one of the Liberty Loan campaigns, and copies were exhibited throughout New England. Caproni sold plasters, and Gorham made a small number of bronze casts (Nos. 36 and 37).[126] *Captured But Not Conquered* is perhaps Dallin's most brilliant essay into the psychological complexities of a subject. One student described it in part: "...With feet firmly braced, one hand is carelessly thrust in his pocket in a happy-go-lucky way that flings defiance in the face of his captors, but the other is tightly clenched and tense at his side which bodes no good to his captors...."[127] Apparently Sergeant Halyburton actually became a prison camp hero by demanding more humane treatment for the Americans from their captors.

Any candid discussion of Dallin's work must acknowledge that in repeating motifs too often he reduced them to visual cliches; this is especially true of his supplicant figures. After his interpretation of inner strength in *Captured But Not Conquered*, the statue *Mine Eyes*

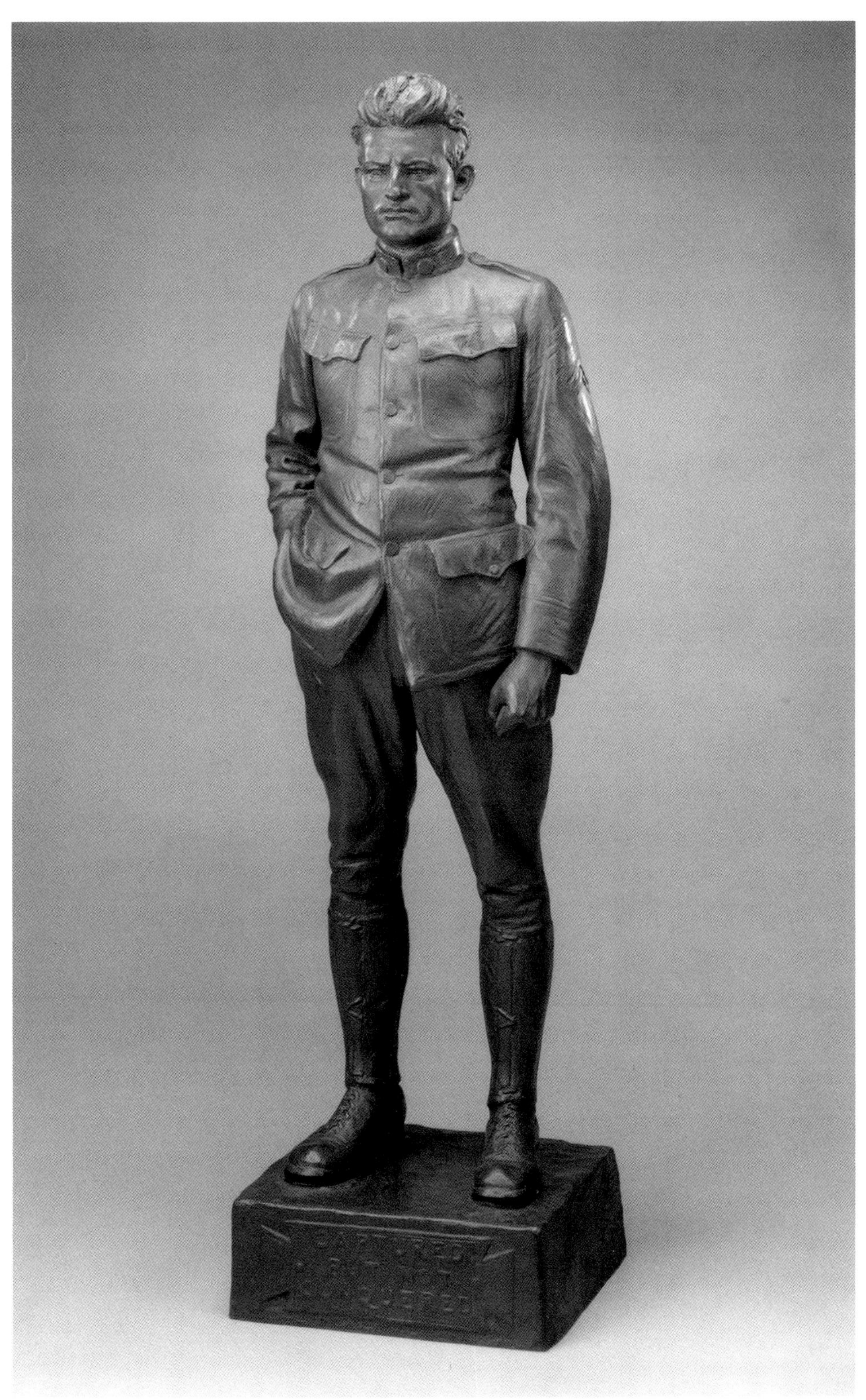

No. 37. Dallin. *Captured But Not Conquered*.

Have Seen the Glory (No. 38) seems melodramatic, although that weakness is compensated for by the skillful modeling of the surface textures. The Secretary of the Interior remarked at its exhibition in Washington, "...He has done his task abroad and his sleeves are rolled back ready for the great challenge of this country. He is young America...."[128]

* * * * *

Dallin made a number of models for World War I memorials and other commemorative monuments that were not placed, but exist as photographic records. Ideal in nature, these models typically incorporate classically robed female figures—more often than not holding

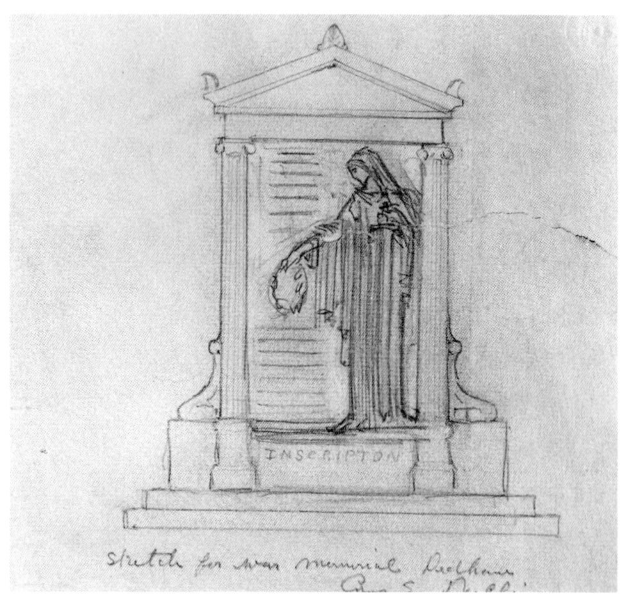

No. 39. Dallin. *Sketch for War Memorial, Dedham.*

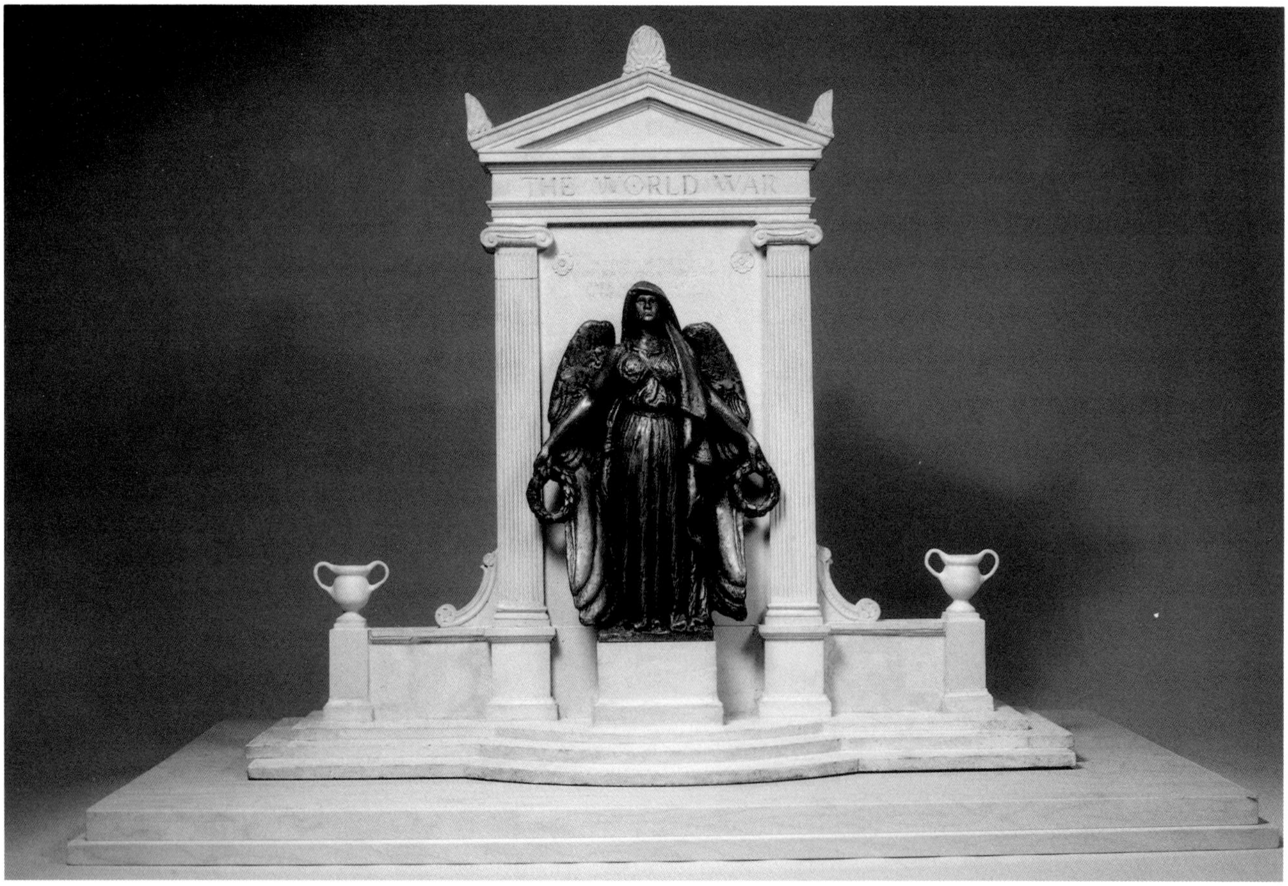

No. 40. Dallin. *Model of a World War I Memorial for Arlington.*

laurel wreaths—standing in front of decorated architectural superstructures. His *Sketch for War Memorial, Dedham* (No. 39) is one of the few known drawings for such a memorial. Equally rare is Dallin's only known surviving model for a World War I memorial (No. 40), which was intended to honor the soldiers from Arlington who had died. The model is well thought out both in terms of the figure and the architecture, and it raises a question about the extent of control Dallin maintained for an overall design when he was collaborating with an architect. This particular design was not erected, but in the case of actual commissions that were carried out, such drawings and models usually remained the property of the artist.

One classically inspired monument that was erected is *Memory* (1924) (Fig. 21) in Sherborn, Massachusetts, which was given by William B. H. Dowse to commemorate those of its sons who had fallen in North America's wars. William W. Dinsmore designed the architecture. The monument was dedicated as part of the town's two-hundred-fiftieth anniversary celebration: "...The figure...is that of a woman, with downcast face in an attitude of pensive remembrance of the sons of Sherborn.... The subject is linked with the recent great conflict by a trench hat, wreathed with a chaplet of laurel, which the figure holds in her encircling arm."[129] In all of Dallin's memorials, none speaks quite so hauntingly or eloquently to the irrevocable loss death brings.

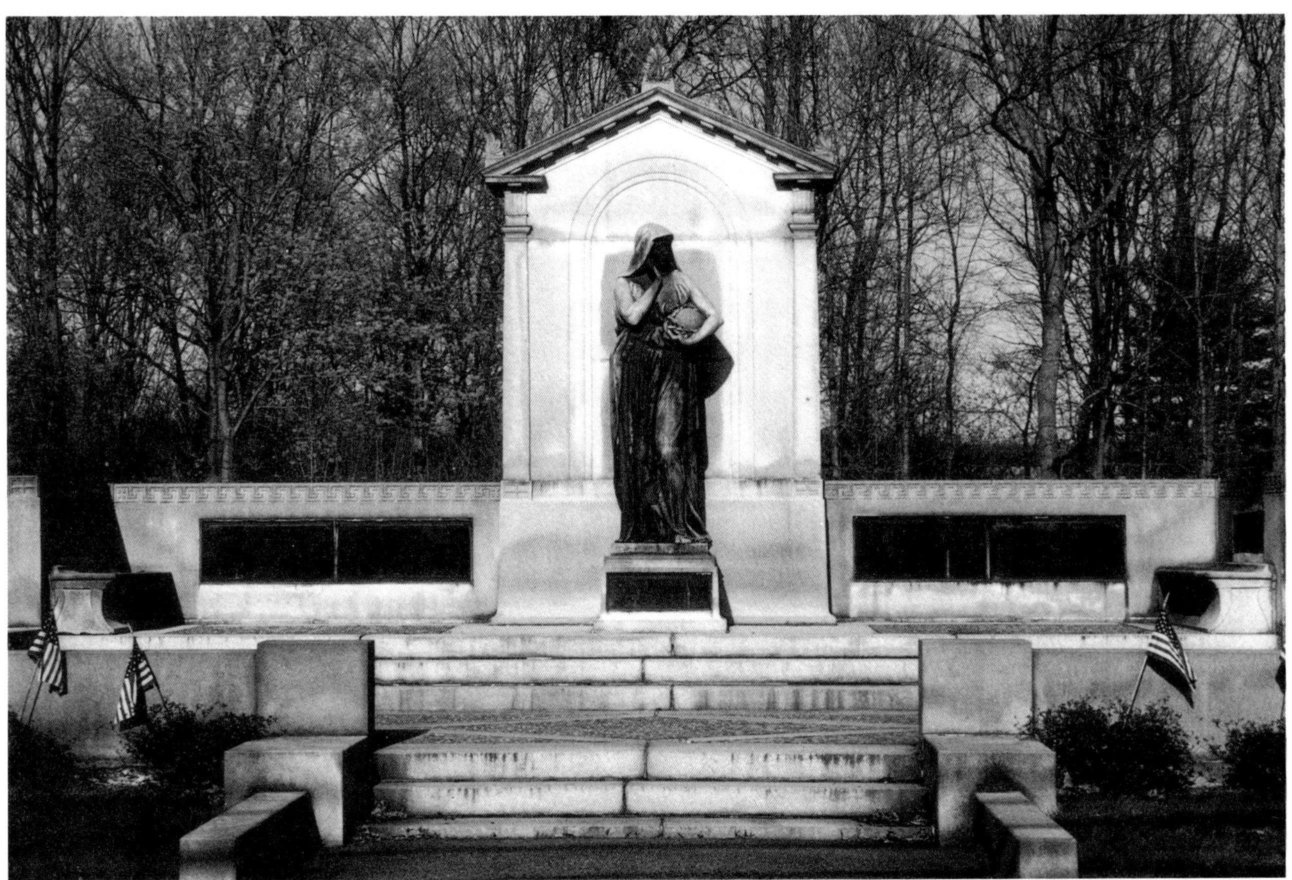

Fig. 21. Dallin. *Memory*. 1924. Sherborn, Massachusetts.

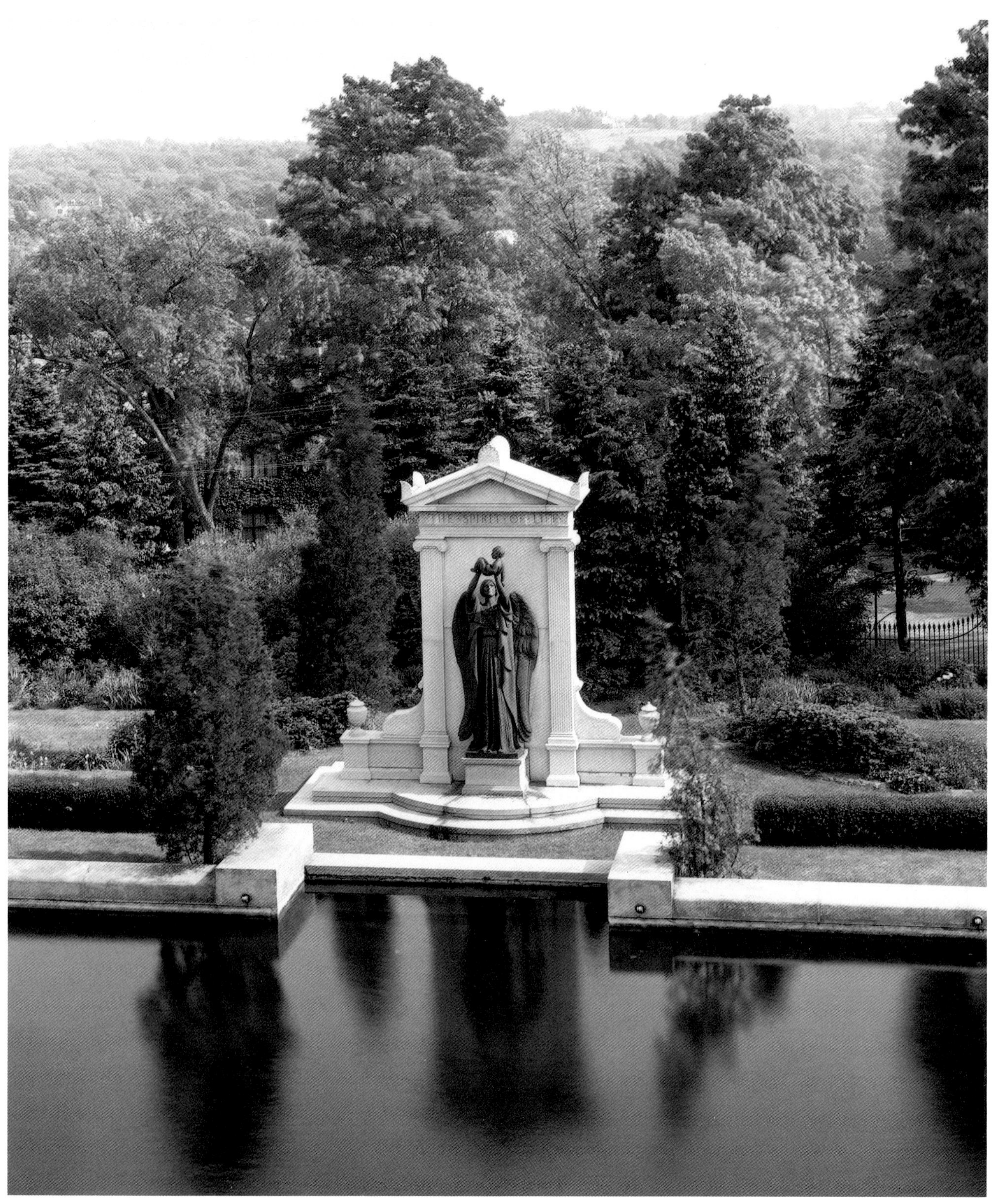

Fig. 23. Dallin. *Spirit of Life*. 1928. Longyear Museum and Historical Society, Brookline, Massachusetts.

John Munro Longyear and his wife, Mary Beecher Longyear, made news c. 1903-06 when they had their elegant stone mansion in Marquette, Michigan, dismantled and rebuilt in Brookline, Massachusetts. In 1927 Mrs. Longyear, who had been widowed in 1922, commissioned Dallin to execute a memorial titled *Spirit of Life* on her Brookline estate. Gay and Proctor designed the marble superstructure, and the local contractor James Driscoll & Sons was responsible for construction.[130] Caproni cast Dallin's figure in plaster, and from it Gorham cast the bronze.[131] Before leaving for Europe in 1928, Dallin wrote Mrs. Longyear, "The bronze cast of the 'Spirit of Life' is all made and is very successful, the marble work on the memorial is in the hands of the architects.... In the fall when I return all the details of the bas relief and inscriptions will be made and the completed memorial should be ready to unveil about the first week in October...."[132] The bas-relief to which Dallin was referring is the double profile portraits of Mrs. Longyear and her deceased husband, which is on the back of the stele, along with the carved names of their children (Fig. 22). Double profile busts on cameos, engraved gems and coins can be traced back to classical times, and the cameo technique enjoyed a renewed popularity in 19th-century England. Also, portraiture on commemorative monuments had a long tradition, especially in Europe, and Mrs. Longyear no doubt would have seen such memorials during her extensive travels. The sensitively modeled plaster version of the portraits is exhibited (No. 41). For the pool side of the monument (Fig. 23), Dallin sculpted a winged and classically garbed figure lifting skyward an infant. The memorial is one of Dallin's finest achievements, and it has been justly compared with Daniel Chester French's Spencer Trask Memorial (1914-15) in Saratoga Springs.[133]

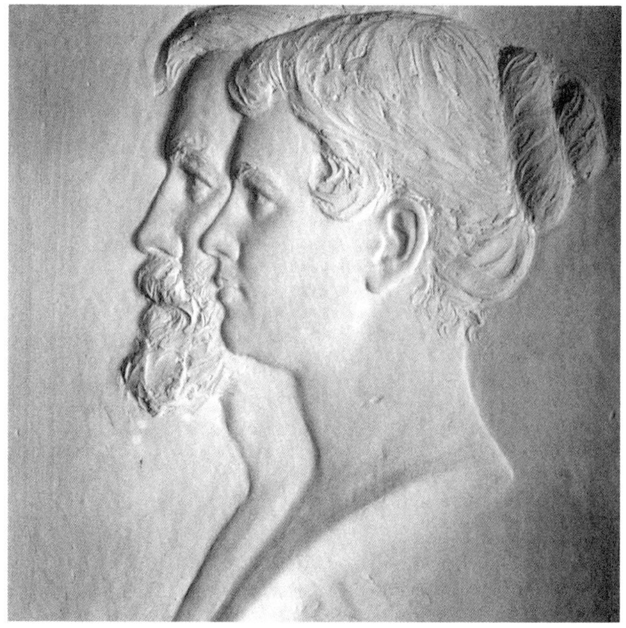

No. 41. Dallin. *Mr. and Mrs. John Munro Longyear.*

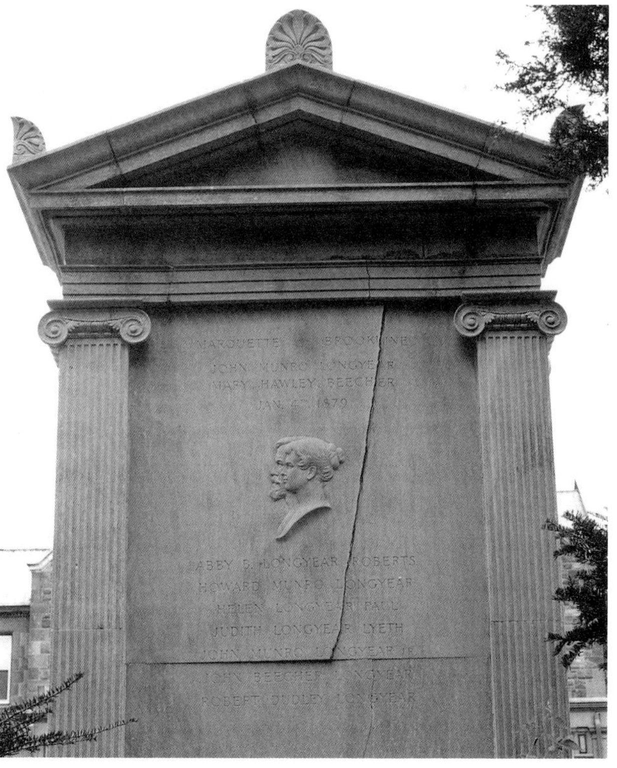

Fig. 22. Dallin. *Mr. and Mrs. John Munro Longyear*, relief portraits on the reverse side of *Spirit of Life*. c. 1928. Longyear Museum and Historical Society, Brookline, Massachusetts.

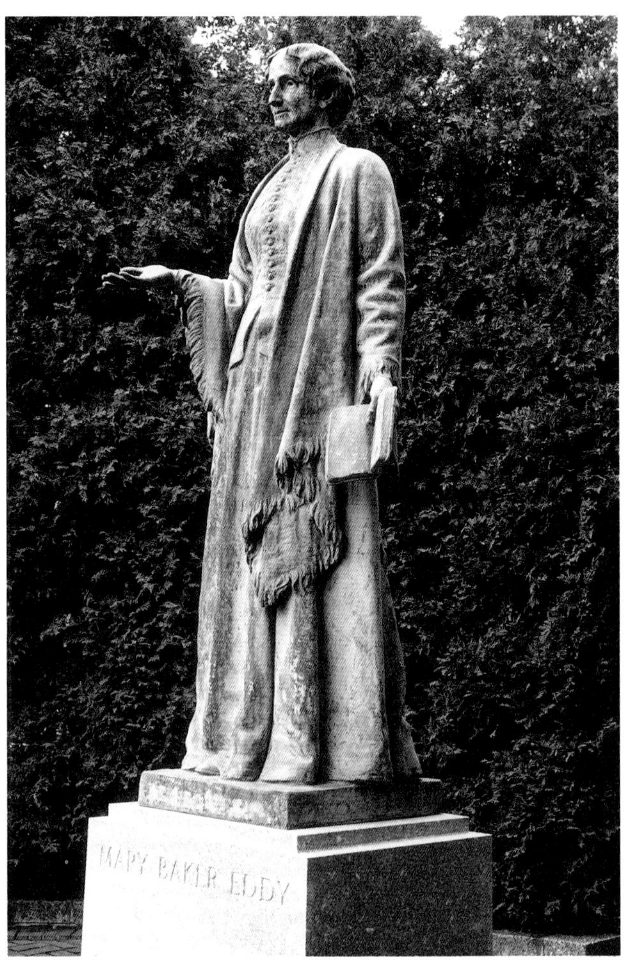

Fig. 24. Dallin. *Mary Baker Eddy*. 1922. Longyear Museum and Historical Society, Brookline, Massachusetts.

Mr. and Mrs. John Munro Longyear followed the tenets of Christian Science, and she was invited to visit with Mary Baker Eddy on several occasions. In 1922 Mrs. Longyear commissioned Dallin to sculpt an over life-size statue of *Mary Baker Eddy* (Fig. 24). After the statue had been cast by Gorham, it was placed in storage until 1966, when it was unveiled by the Longyear Foundation as part of the centennial anniversary of the discovery of Christian Science by Mary Baker Eddy. Mrs. Longyear had intended to place the bronze in a new museum, but she died in 1931 before her plans materialized.[134] The *Quarterly News* commented, "One realizes the fullness of his [Dallin's] achievement when one sees in the statue, not a human Mary Baker Eddy, but the pioneer, teacher, Founder, Leader, combined in one monumental figure...."[135] Dallin animated the figure with somewhat restrained gestures, and his apprenticeship with Jean Dampt is evident in his masterful treatment of the bronze surfaces, especially the jacket and shawl, which suggest detail without closely recorded specifics. Among the most rare and delicate of Dallin's surviving work is a small clay version of the statue (No. 42), which he left with Mrs. Longyear.

* * * * *

The impressive collections of the Springville Museum of Art had their beginning in 1903 when two Utah artists, Cyrus Dallin and the painter John Hafen, each donated one of his works to the local public schools. In 1937 the Hafen-Dallin Club was formed when "...a group of prominent women of Springville met to organize an art club honoring their own native artists...the purpose of the club is to, 'Foster and perpetuate the appreciation and growth of fine arts in this community.'"[136] While the Dallins were traveling in Europe in 1925, the Mothers' Study Club of Springville decided to ask Dallin to sculpt a self-portrait for the high school's art collection. This Dallin agreed to do for the cost of materials, and the bronze (No. 43) was cast in time for its 1927 unveiling.[137] Dallin recorded his own aging features in a direct manner, while avoiding an analysis of his psychological makeup.

Emmeline Wells was a celebrated activist in her day. She led the lobbying efforts for full women's suffrage in the Utah constitution, and she traveled widely lecturing for the rights of women. She and Susan B. Anthony were close personal friends. For forty years she was editor of the *Woman's Exponent*, which represented

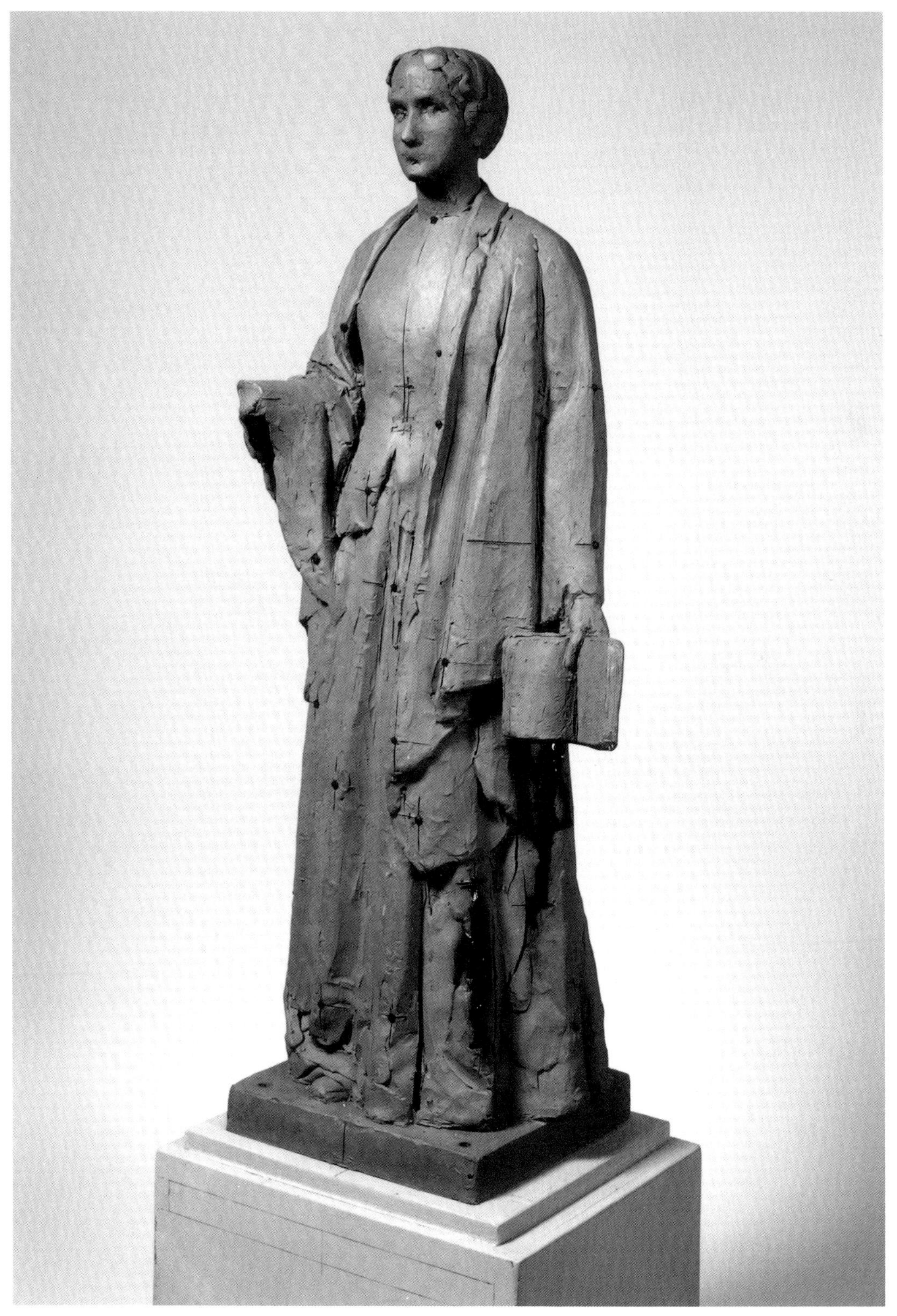

No. 42. Dallin. *Mary Baker Eddy*.

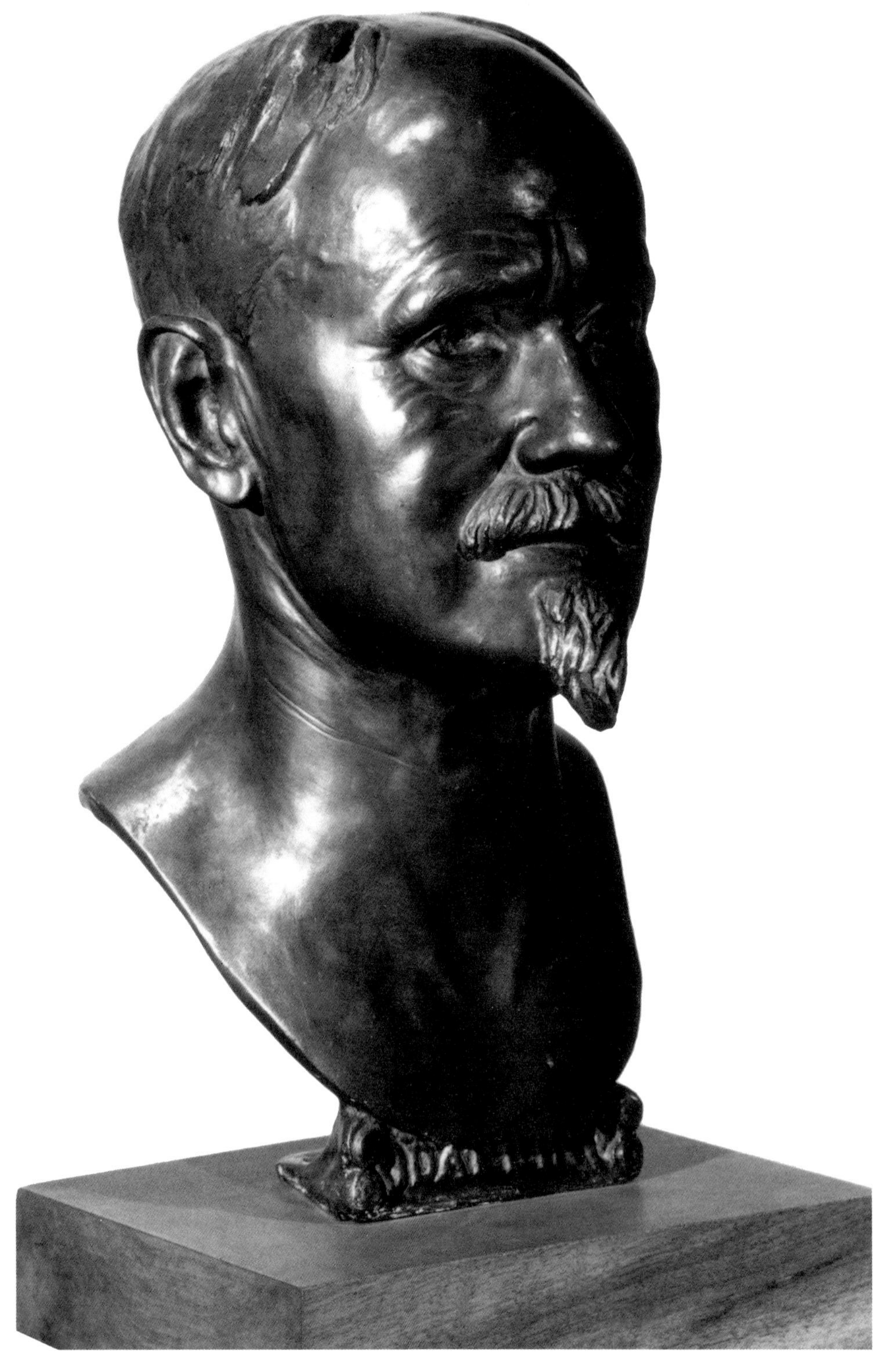

No. 43. Dallin. *Self-Portrait Bust.*

the thinking of many members of The Church of Jesus Christ of Latter-day Saints; this position she resigned in her eighties to become President of the Relief Society. In order to commemorate the centennial anniversary of her birth in 1828, "...Dr. Jane W. Skolfield...called a meeting of the prominent public women throughout the State, with a view of erecting a monument in her honor...from voluntary contributions...."[138] Dallin agreed to model a bust from photographs for $2,000, and the remaining $1,000 that had been raised established a loan fund for senior and graduate women at the University of Utah (No. 44). The over life-size marble bust, which was unveiled in February 1928, occupies a niche in the rotunda of the Utah state capitol; the features are somewhat heavily carved so that the bust would carry visually from its elevated position. While Dallin would have sculpted the model from which the plaster was cast, the marble bust in Salt Lake City would have been carved by stonecutters after his design.[139]

Dallin's last public monument of note in Utah was the Pioneer Mother Memorial, which was dedicated in July 1932 in Springville.[140] The memorial consists of a large bronze bust-length female resting upon a granite base, to which is attached a bronze relief depicting westward migration. The features of the *Pioneer Mother* are those of Dallin's mother, from a marble bust he had executed during her life. Monuments commemorating the heroic pioneer women were popular during the 1920s and 1930s—for instance, the highly publicized *Pioneer Woman* in Ponca City, Oklahoma, and the twelve identical statues titled *The Madonna of the Trail*, which the Daughters of the American Revolution had placed from Maryland to California.

* * * * *

Although the over life-size *Paul Revere* for Boston was young Dallin's first major commission, it turned out to be the last of his public monuments to be erected—in 1940, only a few years before his death. The statue does not sustain his reputation. Just as Washington Allston's *Belshazzar's Feast* (1817-43) had dogged the artist by his inability to complete it, so too was Dallin frustrated for decades by his difficulty with the design for the Revere monument and by the City of Boston's reluctance to fulfill its agreement with him. Allston struggled to bring his picture to a successful completion at a period when large history paintings had lost their public appeal. Dallin finally won his struggle to see the *Paul Revere* erected, but by then the tradition of academic sculpture honoring national heroes had lost its vitality. America's victories in World War II would lead its people to a new view of themselves, and the corresponding changes in the arts marked the end of the public's demand for sculpture in the manner practiced by Cyrus Dallin.

ix

Dallin taught modeling from the antique and life, and composition at the Massachusetts Normal Art School from 1899 until his retirement in 1941.[141] Massachusetts College of Art, as the school is now named, was established in 1873 in response to an 1870 act of the Legislature, which recognized "...the great importance of drawing as a branch of education...." The first catalogue states: "This school is intended as a Training School for the purpose of qualifying teachers and masters of industrial drawing.... In the future it may be necessary to provide for high skill in technical drawing and high art culture...."[142] The esteem that Dallin enjoyed as a teacher is perhaps best reflected in the following tribute to him:

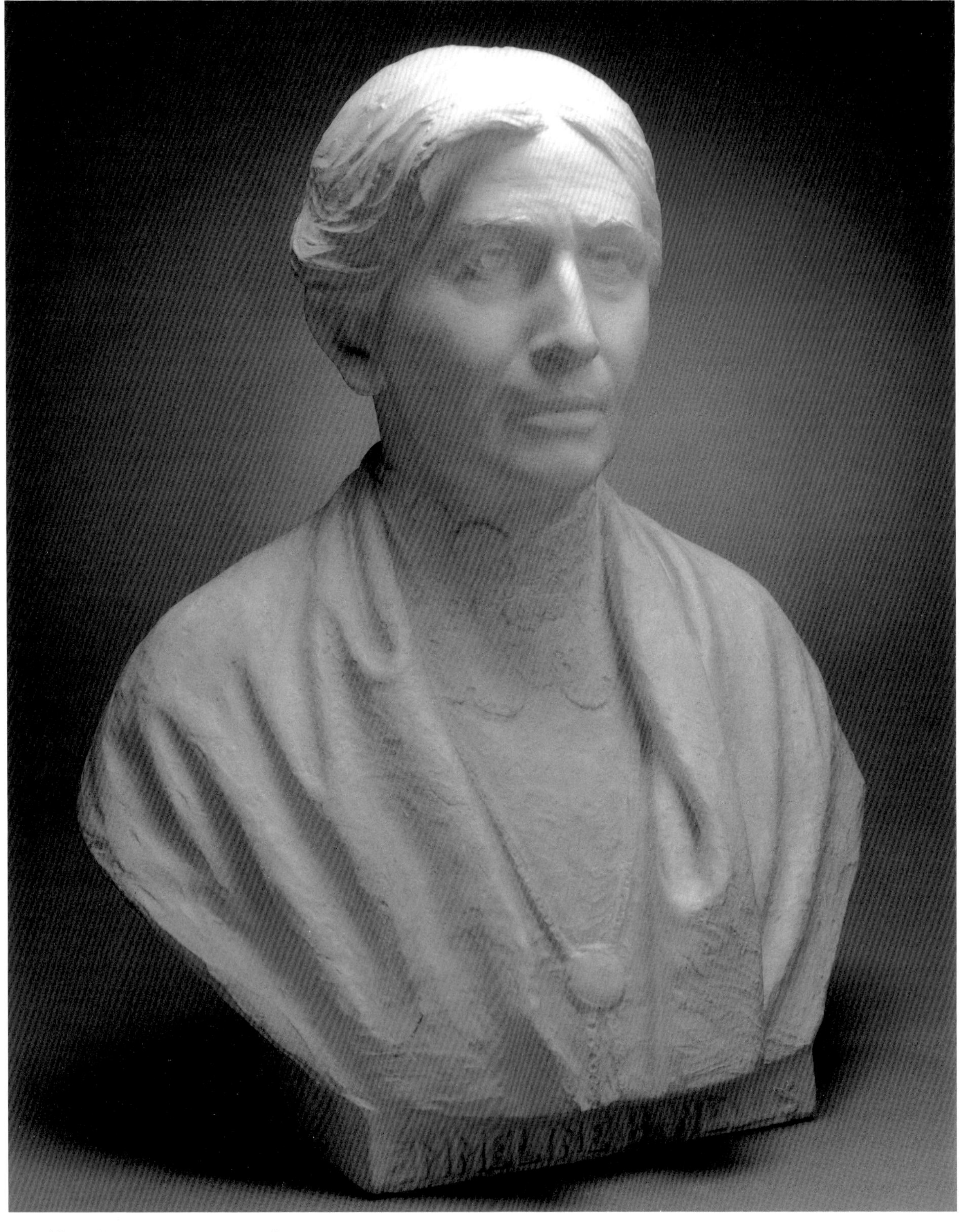

No. 44. Dallin. *Emmeline B. Wells*.

> We, members of the Alumni Association of the Massachusetts School of Art, give this testimonial of love and admiration. You have been for many years a great American artist, and to all who have worked and studied in our school an inspiring teacher. Second to none in any of the Arts, you have immortalized the soul and the tradition of America. In the difficult art of Sculpture you have added great masterpieces to our national Pantheon of monuments. We who have known you intimately can share with the world those masterpieces, while we treasure for ourselves the years of personal inspiration and friendship.[143]

During the years the Dallins lived in Arlington Heights, Mrs. Dallin was very active with community groups, and he frequently lectured and discussed art—plus giving press interviews. On numerous occasions over the years, Dallin lamented that public support for the arts was not increasing. He was an idealist who expressed the thought that a love of beauty could eradicate vandalism and the growth of blighted neighborhoods. He also believed in the value of sculpture as a public asset, and in line with the philosophy of the Beaux-Arts artists, he continued to advocate the embellishment of urban architecture.[144]

While many of his colleagues would not enter sculptural competitions, Dallin did. The comments he made in an interview c. 1902 dealing with the controversy surrounding the General Ulysses S. Grant Memorial in Washington probably reflect not only his dissatisfaction with competitions but more deeply his recent frustration with the Brigham Young Memorial and *Paul Revere*:

> "One who has lived in Europe, and particularly in Paris...is impressed with the artistic dignity of the government competitions held there. The jury is always composed of eminent sculptors.... To a sculptor there is no place of more interest than the Municipal Museum of Paris, in which are exhibited all the sketches, cartoons and models of the public works of Paris. Here are seen the three models that have won the first three prizes offered for designs of a great number of the statues that...now adorn the city of Paris.... Though my own good countrymen have been kind to me, awarding me a first-class medal at the Chicago World's fair and medals at the Pan-American and other expositions, my treatment from the French artists and the honors received at the salon and from the French government at the Paris exposition have made me feel that there is one place in the world where I have received sympathetic recognition...."[145]

In the article "American Sculpture. Its Present Aspects and Tendencies," he commented further on the importance of French art on the American sculptural tradition:

> We inherited our ideas of plastic art...from England, and John Flaxman, Canova and Thorwaldsen were naturally the inspiration of the first American sculptors.... Power's Greek Slave with all its sentimental inanity was the logical outcome of this so-called classic spirit.... These men lost sight of the fact that the only way to appreciate and understand Greek art is to study nature in the Greek spirit.... In speaking of American sculpture we must confess that it is preeminently a reflection of the sculpture of France and that it has not yet acquired a national character.... The famous French sculptor, M. Fremiet, said to me one day...that the French

> were looking to America to develop a national art destined not only to equal but to surpass their own....[146]

The irony is that when American sculpture moved into its own it supplanted the academic tradition.

Judging by his comments about Henri Matisse, whose work he did not like, Dallin probably would not have approved of the direction painting and sculpture have taken since the 1940s: "...I hear students raving about...Matisse, and, if this Matisse is a fair representative of the new art, I am afraid it is doomed to become a sort of asylum for the inefficient...."[147] At the same time, he expressed a deep appreciation of the art of Native Americans as well as that of other cultures: "'A more highly developed civilization except that it gives greater means to gratify our emotional whims does not necessarily mean that there is any higher appreciation of art. The primitive peoples of the world have been the greatest lovers of art....'"[148] He also admired the art of the Orient: "Our most accomplished colorists have a most serious admiration for the perfect coloring of the richly endowed Chinese. Our ablest draughtsmen acknowledge the magnificent power of abstraction that was displayed by the national artists of Japan."[149]

In reply to Ralph Adams Cram's challenge to colleges to "train men for leadership," Dallin "...pointed out the necessity of an emotional reaction if truth is to be realized...."[150] Perhaps nowhere did Dallin more clearly articulate the importance of an emotional response to art than in his comments to Seaton-Schmidt about Auguste Rodin: "'I always strive to express some emotion because I believe that to be the only thing which constitutes art.... Unless a statue, a picture expresses something...I consider it useless. Now Rodin possesses emotion and the power of communicating it to his work.... Nearly all French sculptors make the external, the appearance, very perfect...but they lack Rodin's powers of perception and expression; he sees and understands more profoundly; he gives us life. That is because he works as the Greeks worked, from Nature; he is their legitimate descendant. Rodin, Michelangelo, the Greeks!'"[151]

NOTES

CYRUS E. DALLIN: HIS SMALL BRONZES AND PLASTERS

1. See Michael Edward Shapiro, *Cast and Recast. The Sculpture of Frederic Remington,* National Museum of American Art (Washington, D.C., 1981; second printing, Amon Carter Museum, Fort Worth, 1990), 13-35.

2. Tom Armstrong, et al., *200 Years of American Sculpture,* (New York, 1976), 136-37, and Michael Edward Shapiro, *Bronze Casting and American Sculpture, 1850-1900* (Newark, Delaware, 1985), 102-03.

3. Text information and a copy of a typed ms. related to the Caproni history is courtesy of Robert Shure, President, Skylight Studios Inc. & Giust Gallery: "For the past thirty years Lino Giust has owned and operated what remains of P. P. Caproni & Brother Plaster Arts, the company that was nationally known at the turn of the century for museum quality plaster casts of antique and classical sculptures.... Lino occupies the original Caproni building.... the 4500 square foot 2 story sky-lit space remains the stage for exact copies of the Parthenon and *Cantoria Friezes*; full size statues of Donatello's *St. George* and Michelangelo's head of *David....*"

4. The most thoroughly documented study of Dallin is Rell G. Francis, *Cyrus E. Dallin. Let Justice Be Done* (Springville, Utah, 1976): in conjunction with the book's publication, there was an exhibition of Dallin's work at the Springville Museum of Art. A number of articles published during Dallin's life remain sources of information: William Howe Downes, "Cyrus E. Dallin, Sculptor," *Brush and Pencil,* V (October 1899), [1]-18 [reprinted with slight variations in New England Magazine, 21 (October 1899), 196-209], [file copies Museum of Fine Arts, Boston (MFA,B), and Dartmouth College, respectively]; James Spencer Dickerson, "Cyrus E. Dallin and his Indian Sculpture," *The Monumental News* [1909], 679-81, [file copy MFA,B]; M. Stannard May, "The Work of Cyrus E. Dallin," *New England Magazine,* 48 (November 1912), 408-15, [file copy Dartmouth]; E. Wilbur Pomeroy, "Cyrus E. Dallin and the North American Indian," *Arts and Decoration,* 4 (February 1914), 152-53; A. Seaton-Schmidt, "An American Sculptor: Cyrus E. Dallin," [The International Studio, 58 (1916)], 109-14, [file copy Smithsonian Institution]; Katherine Thayer Hodges, "Dallin the Sculptor, His Indian Stories in Marble," *The American Magazine of Art,* XV (October 1924), 521-27; E. Waldo Long, "Dallin, Sculptor of Indians," *The World's Work,* LIV (September 1927), [563]-68. Most of the large collection of material related to Dallin at the Robbins Library (RL), Arlington, Massachusetts, is available on microfilm from the Archives of American Art (AAA).

5. Vittoria Colonna Dallin, "The 'Great Spirit' and Cyrus Dallin," undated typed ms., RL.

6. Long, 566. Paragraphs are merged in the quotations of this essay.

7. "Dallin, Autobiographical," a clipping, "Furnished The Tribune by Mrs. Hamilton by courtesy of Mr. Dallin," 1894, AAA 179.

8. Downes, 5, and "Autobiographical." Also, Cyrus E. Dallin, "The Spirit of Life," typed ms., July 1935, RL.

9. See "Bicentennial of Birth of Paul Revere Recalls Competition for Equestrian Statue at Boston," *The Federal Architect* (*January* 1934), 16-7, and "Teacher Was Jealous, Explains Cyrus Dallin," AAA 183.

10. Shapiro, *Cast and Recast,* 32-4.

11. T. H. Bartlett to C. H. Blanchard in Silver City, Utah, January 21[?], 1880. Courtesy Ruth Dallin Stevenson.

12. T. H. Bartlett to Thomas Dallin, June 1, 1880. Courtesy Ruth Dallin Stevenson.

13. Dallin to his parents, October 24, 1880. Courtesy Ruth Dallin Stevenson.

14. In his letter of October 24, 1880 (note 13), Dallin continued in his still uneducated hand: "...I am making some peices of work (to send out home) in Terra Cotta for the purpose of sale the principal peice is a Panthier a reproduction of one of A L Baryes the late great French Animal Sculptor it is about 17 or 18 inches long I shall have it Burned and it will probely fetch about $5^{00} apeice.... I will send the first one that is finished." On November 19, 1880, Dallin wrote D. O. Calder, "I have a mold of my principall peice at the mold makers as I have not had the money to get it out...," and December 23 he wrote his father, "...yesterday I put in [the kiln] 6 Panthers and 9 small tiles...." Courtesy Ruth Dallin Stevenson. According to Dallin ("Autobiographical"), he sold "...quite a number in Boston."

15. Kathryn Greenthal, et al., *American Figurative Sculpture in the Museum of Fine Arts, Boston* (Boston, 1986), 270-[71], (text by Paula M. Kozol).

16. Bartlett wrote to Thomas Dallin, March 3, 1881, "...I believe that a boy should be *independent,* & not dependent on others any more than is absolutely necessary...." On May 3, 1881, Bartlett wrote D. O. Calder: "...The boy needs a thorough drilling in learning how to take care of himself. I do not wish to accept the responsibility of his training without the sanction & advice of his friends.... I have told the father that the best counsel that I could give was that his son should go into the Terra-Cotta works on the premises.... I don't think the boy is particularly anxious to pitch in & do for himself except in the work he likes...." Courtesy Ruth Dallin Stevenson.

17. October 20, 1881, S. H. Morse wrote Dallin's parents, "...I am glad to tell you he [Cyrus] has much improved in health since he came here...." Courtesy Ruth Dallin Stevenson. See "Autobiographical," and Downes, 6.

18. Francis discusses the *Revere* commission in detail, 10-33 and 183-93. Daniel Chester French was another competitor, and in "Spirit of Life," Dallin remarks on his generous nature and their long friendship. See also Margaret French Cresson, Chesterwood, not dated, to Dallin, AAA 141.

19. Typed copies, City of Boston, In Board of Aldermen, March 19, 1883, and Articles of Agreement between Dallin and Hugh O'Brien, July 4, 1885, AAA 183.

20. Augustus Saint-Gaudens to Dallin, January 12, 1887, AAA 141.

21. What little evidence there is suggests that Saint-Gaudens remained polite and helpful toward Dallin, but sometimes reserved—especially when Dallin asked the older artist to intercede with a committee. See Dallin to Saint-Gaudens, January 28, 1892, The Church of Jesus Christ of Latter-day Saints, Historical Department—Archives, and Saint-Gaudens to Dallin, June 27, 1906, Special Collections, Dartmouth College Library, Saint-Gaudens Papers.

22. "The Fine Arts," [December 26, 1899], AAA 183, and "In Hands of a Committee," *The Boston Globe,* January 12, 1900. For an illustration of Dallin's sculpture and the remarks of Professor Charles Eliot Norton, see "Paul Revere Equestrian Statue," *Globe,* January 11, 1900.

23. Dallin signed an Agreement with Pietro Caproni, Treasurer, P. P. Caproni and Brother, February 28, 1907, for plaster casts of *Paul Revere, John Hancock* and the *Medicine Man,* AAA 178. See also P. P. Caproni and Brother, *Caproni Casts. American Indians and Other Sculptures by Cyrus E. Dallin* (Boston, 1915), 3, AAA 179.

24. See *Bronzes and Bronze Casting By the Gorham M'f'g Co.* (Providence, 1893), 34-7, and H. W. Janson, *19th-Century Sculpture* (New York, 1985), 212.

25. Frank R. Arnold, "An American Sculptor of Indians and Soldiers," *Young Woman's Journal*, XXX (June 1919), [291], AAA 179.

26. Dallin's handwritten ms., "Chapu & the Prix de Rome," AAA 2803. See also "Cyrus E. Dallin, Eminent Sculptor, Tells of Career," AAA 179.

27. Janson, 186-87.

28. Downes, 9-10.

29. An unidentified clipping, AAA 179, reads, "...M. Frémiet...took such a lively interest in the Lafayette that he offered to aid our young Boston sculptor by suggestions and criticisms...." The clipping "Dallin's Lafayette—Burne-Jones and the Parisians," AAA 182, comments: "...With the French statuary is Mr. Bartlett's 'Indian Warrior,' a fine...figure, but has it quite the features of a North American Indian? Is it not rather an ancient Gaul? Mr. Dallin's bronze model for...Lafayette cannot fail to be noticed and admired...." Both Truman H. Bartlett and his son, Paul Wayland Bartlett, studied with Frémiet, who befriended many an American artist. Dallin's *Signal of Peace* invites comparison with Frémiet's *Mounted Torchbearer* (1883), Hotel de Ville, Paris.

30. National Museum of American Art files.

31. Numerous sources recount the Rosa Bonheur anecdotes. Downes in the New England Magazine version of his article, 200, identified *Indian Head* as *Head of Sioux Indian*; Francis, 39, titled it *Phillip.*

32. Dallin told Waldo Long, 568: "'The origin of that statue...goes back to my boyhood, to a day when I witnessed a peace pow-wow between the Indian chiefs and the United States Army officers...." In a typed ms., "Bronze Indian Head—Mr. Dallin," 1932, he wrote: "The small head is the study I made for my first equestrian statue.... Having received permission, I immediately set to work and selected a fine, upstanding young Sioux...by the name of Philip Kick Bear.... My work consisted of making what may be termed a small sketch model of the design that I had worked out, called 'The Signal of Peace,' representing...the

first contact of the Indian with the White Man.... I asked Monsieur [Jules] Dalou, who had a studio nearby, if he would kindly come in and give me some criticism.... He looked at the statue [*Signal of Peace*] and said, 'My friend, I do not like the posture of the Indian...he is sitting down all sort of crouched with his back bent and that to my mind is not the proper position for a fine equestrian statue.'... after he left I...said to myself, 'I guess Monsieur Dalou never saw an Indian on horseback.'..." Courtesy Ruth Dallin Stevenson. Dallin's keen sense of observation is seen to advantage by comparing an early untitled painting of his showing an Indian chief and the Springville mountains and a photograph by Edward S. Curtis titled *In the Bad Lands*: see Francis, fig. 36, and Florence Curtis Graybill and Victor Boesen, *Edward Sheriff Curtis. Visions of a Vanishing Race* (New York, 1981), [133].

33. William A. Coffin, "The Columbian Exposition.—I. Fine Arts: French and American Sculpture," *The Nation*, 57 (August 3, 1893), 81.

34. "His Signal of Peace," [Chicago Tribune, June 10, 1894], AAA 183.

35. John Nicholson, "The Statue of Moroni" (subtitle), *Deseret Evening News*, April 6, 1892; also Albert L. Zobell, Jr., "Cyrus Dallin and the Angel Moroni Statue," *Improvement Era* (April 1968), 4, AAA 179.

36. The information that Dallin made a large model of *Moroni* cannot be confirmed: see Francis, 67-8, and Florence S. and Jack Sears, "How We Got the Angel Moroni Statue," *The Instructor* (October 1953), 293. "The Temple...," *The Salt Lake Herald*, October 4, 1891, reads: "...The figure of the angel...is presented herewith. It is from a design made by Dallin...and now ready for exhibition in the coming Fair. The model in plaster is only 40 inches high, but the bronze figure itself will measure thirteen feet in heighth. The model is to be sent at once to a factory in Salem, O., where the figure will be made of hammered copper...." In "The Temple...," *The Salt Lake Herald*, April 3, 1892, the writer commented, "...He made a small mould in plaster, which was sent to a firm in the East, and they made the copper figure...."

37. *Salt Lake Herald*, April 3, 1892. Scrap Book, Sponsored by the Hafen-Dallin Art Club, Springville Museum of Art: a typed letter (fragment), Utah State Historical Society, April 3, 1940, to Ada M. Barron reads, "...The idea conveyed by the statue is that of a herald...an embodiment of the fact of Moroni bringing the Gospel to the earth in this latter-day dispensation...." Dallin wrote to a Mr. Young, July 30, 1938 (LDS Historical Division—Archives), "...concerning 'what I had in mind'...permit me to state that I had no other thought in mind but to carry out (as best I could) my commission, which was for a statue of the *Mormon Angel 'Moroni.'*"

38. See The Words of Mormon, 8:14 and 10:2, in The Book of Mormon.

39. "Joseph Smith—History. Extracts From the History of Joseph Smith, The Prophet," *The Pearl of Great Price* (Salt Lake City, 1986), 1:32-33, and 1:59-60.

40. The drawings referred to are in the collections of the Museum of Church History and Art, Salt Lake City. "The Mountain of the Lord's House. Construction of the Salt Lake Temple, 1853-1893," an exhibition (March 1993-February 1994) that was organized by Robert O. Davis, Senior Curator of Art, Museum of Church History and Art, presented visitors an instructive view of the Temple's construction. See Armstrong, plate 21.

41. Information courtesy Eldred G. Smith and Robert O. Davis.

42. Articles of Agreement between Dallin and the Brigham Young Memorial Association, April 8, 1892. LDS Historical Department—Archives.

43. *National Sculpture Society Constitution and List of Members* (New York, 1894), 5. See also *Third Exhibition of the National Sculpture Society* (New York, 1898), [5]-16, and Armstrong, 114.

44. *Catalogue of the Exhibition of the National Sculpture Society Under the Auspices of the Municipal Art Society of Baltimore* (n.p., 1908), 25 (remarks by Lorado Taft); Kathryn Greenthal, *Augustus Saint-Gaudens, Master Sculptor* (New York, 1985), 153.

45. On December 13, 1895, Dallin wrote to Heber M. Wells, who was Secretary of the Brigham Young Memorial Association, Salt Lake City: "...It [Library] is very beautiful, and I think is one of the most satisfactory public buildings in the country.... I am enjoying my teaching at the Drexel Institute, as I have pretty much my own way." LDS Historical Division—Archives. See Herbert Small, *Handbook of the New Library of Congress* (Boston, 1901), 64-6.

46. See Vittoria C. Dallin, "Charles Grafly's Work," *New England Magazine. An Illustrated Monthly*, new series, 25 (September 1901-February 1902), 228-35, and Grafly to Mrs. Dallin, May 1, 1901, AAA 180. Mrs. Dallin was herself a woman of intelligence and ability.

47. *Drexel Institute of Art, Science, and Industry, Philadelphia. Annual Catalogue of Students with Introduction, and Officers of Administration and Instruction. 1899-1900*, 1. Mary T. MacAlister, Curator, "Museum Department," *Drexel Institute of Art, Science, and Industry, Philadelphia. Year Book of the Departments and Courses of Instruction. 1897-98*, 205: "The formation of a museum of fine and industrial art was part of the original scheme...as approved by its founder...."

48. Edward D. McDonald and Edward M. Hinton, *Drexel Institute of Technology. 1891-1941* (Philadelphia, 1942), 37 and 122.

49. *Drexel Institute of Art, Science, and Industry, Philadelphia. James MacAlister, LL.D., President. Department of Fine and Applied Art. 1896-97*, 2-3. *Drexel Institute. Yearbook. 1895-96* [on spine of library copy] does not list Fine and Applied Arts courses.

50. See McDonald, 37-8, 125 and 130. In 1894 The School of Illustration was established under Howard Pyle, who taught there until his resignation in 1900. Grafly resigned in 1899, and, although its breakup was made inevitable not only by faculty resignations but also by competition from classes at the Pennsylvania Academy of the Fine Arts, the Fine and Applied Arts continued until 1905, when the trustees announced their termination.

51. Dallin to Heber M. Wells, who was now Utah's Governor, June 8, 1896. LDS Historical Division—Archives.

52. See Maurice Rheims, *19th Century Sculpture* (New York, 1977), 88, 362 and 407 for a discussion of Jean-Auguste Dampt.

53. Dallin to Governor Wells, March 4, 1899. LDS Historical Division—Archives.

54. Dallin, 69 Oakland Avenue, Arlington Heights, Massachusetts, October 28, 1900, to Governor Wells: "I have been having a great trouble with my eyes lately and I haven't done any work for nearly two months.... I have bought a house and some land and am building a studio...." LDS Historical Division—Archives.

55. "Spirit of Life," Dallin's ms. Variations on the train anecdote, and Dallin's chance encounter years later with one of the Native Americans can be found throughout literature on the artist.

56. Alvan F. Sanborn, "Mr. Dallin in Paris," *Boston Evening Transcript*, April 17, 1909. See also in the *Transcript,* "Cyrus Dallin's 'The Appeal to the Great Spirit,'" June 26, 1909, AAA 181. Dickerson, 679-81, illustrated the four equestrians, but did not discuss them as a unity. John V. Sears, "'The Medicine Man' by Dallin," September 29, 1900, saw the *Signal of Peace* and *Medicine Man* as complementary compositions (Historical Society of Pennsylvania, [HSP]).

57. May, 414, and *Museum of Fine Arts Bulletin*, XI (February 1913), 13-4.

58. See among others: John C. Ewers, "Cyrus E. Dallin. Master Sculptor of the Plains Indian," *Montana the Magazine of Western History*, XVIII (January 1968), 38-41; Wayne Craven, *Sculpture in America*, new and revised ed. (Newark, Delaware, 1984), 528-30; Patricia Janis Broder, *Bronzes of the American West* (New York, n.d.), 94-8.

59. Chandler Rathfon Post, *A History of European and American Sculpture*, vol. II (Cambridge, 1921), 251, mentions the *Scout* but not the *Protest* in alluding to Dallin's equestrians. See Francis, 35-63, and also his discussion "The Epic of the Indian," in the pamphlet *Project Tribute,* Springville Museum of Art. For a discussion of Dallin's work see Armstrong, [139] (ill. 195 is incorrectly identified as *The Scout*), and Beatrice Gilman Proske, *Brookgreen Gardens Sculpture,* new ed. (Brookgreen Gardens, 1968), 24-6. *On the Warpath* (No. 15) is listed in Leslie Hindman Auctioneers, *The Arthur Rubloff Collection of American and European Sculpture,* May 22, 1994, no. 7; see also Sotheby Parke Bernet Los Angeles, *Paintings, Drawings and Sculpture from the Collection of The University of Southern California*, May 3, 1982, no. 84. See John E. D. Trask, ed., and J. Nilsen Laurvik, *Catalogue De Luxe of the Department of Fine Arts Panama-Pacific International Exposition*, 2 vols., vol. 2 (San Francisco, n.d.), 434: *On the War Path* was one of the bronzes exhibited by Dallin.

60. Belle Wilde Hooper, June 20, 1956, to Relief Society, Belle Wilde Hooper Scrapbook, LDS Historical Division—Archives.

61. "Cyrus Dallin, Sculptor, Who Gave 'The Scout' to World of Art, A Visitor," [Kansas City Journal, December 3, 1915], AAA 182.

62. Clipping, [Arlington Daily News, October 13, 1931], AAA 184.

63. "Indian Treaties 'Scraps of Paper,'" AAA 180.

64. "Cyrus Dallin Dreams Great Memorial to American Indian...," *Boston Sunday Advertiser*, November 22, 1925, AAA 184.

65. I wish to thank Daniel C. Swan, Senior Curator, Gilcrease Museum, and George Horse Capture, Deputy Assistant Director for Cultural Resources, National Museum of the American Indian, for sharing

with me their thoughts concerning Dallin's sculpture of Native American subjects.

66. Clement E. Conger, et al., *Treasures of State. Fine and Decorative Arts in the Diplomatic Reception Rooms of the U.S. Department of State* (New York, 1991), 468 (text by Wayne Craven).

67. Downes, 16 and 18; telegram, Arthur Krupp, Berndorf, to Dallin, January 10, 1901, AAA 180; Krupp to Dallin, January 11, 1901, AAA 141. See also clippings, AAA 182.

68. Lorado Taft, "American Sculpture at the Exposition, I.," *Brush and Pencil*, VI (July 1900), 166-68, and *The History of American Sculpture* (New York, 1903), 496-500. Charles H. Caffin admired Dallin's ability to combine naturalism with the poetry of the Native American: "'The Stone Age' and 'The Medicine Man,'" HSP.

69. Craven, *Sculpture*, 529. "Plan for the 'Scout' Fund," [Kansas City Times, February 8, 1917], AAA 182, reads: "...Almost all other equestrian statues merely celebrate the deeds of individuals in their lifetime, such as monarchs and warriors...."

70. Fairmount Park Art Association, *Sculpture of a City: Philadelphia's Treasures in Bronze and Stone* (New York, 1974), 210. Also see Penny Balkin Bach, *Public Art in Philadelphia* (Philadelphia, 1992), 209. The statue was cast by Gruet in Paris.

71. Fairmount Park Art Association, *Thirty-Second Annual Report of the Board of Trustees....* (Philadelphia, 1904), 47. Reference the plaster version, see typed letter to Andrew Bolger, November 28, 1903, HSP.

72. David R. Francis, *The Universal Exposition of 1904* (Saint Louis, 1913), 522, Anthropology: "At the Exposition were assembled numerous types of many of the primitive races of the earth.... A group of African pygmies, some of them of man-eating tribes, brought the collection of primitive races down to the lowest known human stage; the Ainus and Patagonians represented the semi-civilized savages still existing like our Indians in countries dominated by highly civilized races and like the Indians rapidly disappearing. In the still exhibits of Anthropology the visitor saw further significant evidences of the slow, tedious evolution of civilization...." For attitudes toward Native Americans see Brian W. Dippie, *The Vanishing American. White Attitudes and U.S. Indian Policy* (Lawrence, Kansas, 1982). Also see Lois Marie Fink, *American Art at the Nineteenth-Century Paris Salons* (New York, 1990), 180-96.

73. David Francis, *Exposition.* 197-200; Craven, *Sculpture,* 469-71. Dallin exhibited four objects: *Official Catalogue of Exhibitors. Universal Exposition, St. Louis, U.S.A., 1904, Division of Exhibits...Art*, revised ed., (Saint Louis, 1904), 59.

74. David Francis, *Exposition,* 200: Remington's rowdy *Four Cowboys Off the Trail* was present at the east entrance as "...an appropriate symbol of greeting."

75. Ibid., 201.

76. Ibid., 201. For whatever the reason, Dallin did not have the large *Sioux Chief,* which is the most agitated of his equestrian figures, cast in bronze. In a lost work titled *Greaser* and an early version of *Paul Revere* (see Francis, *Dallin*, figs. 28 and 29), he experimented with similarly posed mounts. Dallin's *Sioux Chief* anticipates Proctor's bronze *On the War Trail* (1920) for the Denver Civic Center.

77. *National Sculpture Society Catalogue* (1908), 37. Kozol, in Greenthal, *Figurative Sculpture,* [277], writes that a half life-size plaster was exhibited. In the clipping "The Work of American Sculptors" [Boston Transcript, April 8, 1908], Leila Mechlin referred to the *Appeal* in Baltimore as "...Dallin's heroic statue...," AAA 184.

78. "Cyrus Dallin's 'The Appeal to the Great Spirit,'" *Boston Evening Transcript*, June 26, 1909, and "National Academy Opens" [New York Evening Post, December 9, 1911], both AAA 181.

79. *Museum of Fine Arts Bulletin* (February 1913), 13-4. For clippings related to the purchase of the *Appeal*, see especially AAA 181.

80. "Spirit of Life," Dallin's ms.

81. Lengthy ms. material related to the copyright suits is found in AAA 179. See Francis, 44-5, and "The Appeal to the Great Spirit," AAA 181: according to tradition, Dallin's statue was once as popular and widely reproduced as Auguste Bartholdi's *Statue of Liberty*.

82. Ivers Louise Ashley wrote the words and music for *America's "Appeal to the Great Spirit,"* copyright 1929, (first verse): "Hear Thou, O God, a Nation's supplication! Keep, strengthen, lead us thru the years to come. Thou our Protector from what e'er betide, Safely we journey if Thou wilt be our Guide." In an unidentified clipping, "Finds His Answer in Dallin's Work," President John Cousens of Tufts College related how he explained the meaning of religion to a student by taking him to see Dallin's statue. Both RL.

83. *Sculpture and Mural Paintings ...Panama-Pacific International Exposition at San Francisco, 1915* (San Francisco, 1915), frontispiece. Laurvik discusses American sculpture in *Catalogue De Luxe*, Trask, ed., vol. 1, 51-60.

84. Frank Titus, clipping [Kansas City Times, February 8, 1917], Missouri Valley Special Collections, Kansas City Public Library. See Giles Carroll Mitchell, *There Is No Limit: Architecture and Sculpture in Kansas City* (Kansas City, 1934), 46-50, and Municipal Art Commission, *A Survey of Kansas City's Public Outdoor Art* (Kansas City, 1977), 36. The *Scout* was vandalized but has been conserved.

85. Dallin to William K. Bixby, September 18, 1917, W. K. Bixby Papers, Missouri Historical Society. See Stella G. S. Perry, with an introduction by A. Stirling Calder, Acting Chief of Sculpture, *The Sculpture and Mural Decorations of the Exposition....* (San Francisco, n.d.), 168: "...He [Dallin] says that this Scout is to be the last of his long series of Indian studies, and he believes it to be the best.... It has a clear and beautiful directness that is almost Greek in feeling...."

86. Roman Bronze Works Archives, page 267 related to Dallin, Amon Carter Museum, and Binderbook: Gorham Bronze—Statuary—List of Royalties, Manuscript Department, John Hay Library, Brown University. A Roman Bronze cast of *Medicine Man* is in the collections of The Saint Louis Museum of Art. The subject was sold in plaster by Caproni. See George Gurney's foreword, 6-7, in Shapiro, *Cast and Recast*, and Charles H. Carpenter, Jr., *Gorham Silver, 1831-1981* (New York, 1982), 154-55, for the relative degrees of authenticity in bronze casts. For recent posthumous casts of Dallin's Native American subjects, see The Taggart Group, Las Vegas, *The American Indian* (n.p., n.d.).

87. See Binderbook: Gorham, Brown University, and The Heckscher Museum, *Catalogue of the Collection. Painting and Sculpture* (Huntington, New York, 1979), 17-8 (text by Ronald G. Pisano). *Signal of Peace* was cast by Caproni c. 1920: see Agreement, September 7, 1920, AAA 178.

88. Binderbook: Gorham, Brown University; according to Charles E. Baxley, June 22, 1979, to B. Maneckji, Textron Inc., versions of Dallin's *Scout* were registered for copyright March 30, 1910, and January 15, 1912. Dallin signed an Agreement with Caproni for *The Scout* in January 1912, AAA 178, and a 38-inch version was advertised in the 1915 catalogue, 4.

89. Agreement between Dallin and Gardiner M. Lane, President, Museum of Fine Arts, Boston, December 23, 1912, AAA 178.

90. Binderbook: Gorham, Brown University. See also Carpenter, *Gorham,* 153, and Conger, *Treasures of State,* 468, for Dallin's 1916 agreement with Gorham. See among the Gorham records at Brown University a ms. book, identified by a slip of paper as "Identification Assigned to Statuary & Bronzes 1906-1930," inside of which is attached a typed five page ms. (c. 1947-48), which reads in part: "Back in the year 1905 on small bronzes fabricated or cast by the Bronze Division...a system of designations was established giving to each article a 'Q' number. One series of numbers started with Q-1 and through the years includes numbers over Q-600 and in most cases these items were items cast or fabricated by the Company for stock. The other series of numbers or letters started with number QAA and such letters were customarily given to productions which the Gorham Company cast for customers such as sculptors.... In both series of numbers and letters, certain articles which had sales appeal were cast by the Gorham Foundries as stock items and sold as such.... In case a plaster model, through repeated usage in making castings, should become in need of repairs it has been customary in previous years for us to write the sculptor and inform him of the circumstances and request him to repair the models. Where it seems probable that any subsequent casting in bronze will be made, we have recommended to the sculptor that he order a metal pattern made...." Another typed ms. at Brown dated October 27, 1945, "Small Statuary Bronzes," identifies four categories of bronzes: "...*CONSIGNMENT BRONZE* - models owned by Sculptor - cast. on sculpture orders paid for - Put consignment sale in Gorham customer galleries at price determined by Sculptor.... *ROYALTY BRONZE* - models owned by Sculptor loaned to Gorham with the right to cast any number of duplicates, and to sell...at Gorham's determined sales price. Gorham to pay sculptor *set* royalty.... *GORHAM OWNED BRONZE*...models purchased outright by Gorham.... *SMALL BRONZE* - cast to order for Sculptor on special order and delivered in ordered quantity to sculptor - Gorham has no right to reproduce, without Sculptor's permission." See also typed ms. dated January 3, 1945, for Gorham's method of distribution. September 21, 1994, Rhonda L. Butler, Textron Inc., showed a number of unassembled Gorham bronzes of Dallin's work to Jonathan L. Fairbanks, Robert Shure, Rebecca Reynolds and Kent Ahrens: although a visual examination of these bronzes is not conclusive in itself, it is believed that they may be metal patterns used in the casting process (see No. 45). A plaster version of the *Appeal to the Great Spirit* much like the one in this exhibition (No. 12) would have been the original casting model for the bronze in this size. Unfortunately, the history of the Rockwell Museum's plaster cannot be traced (Douglas Allen wrote to Robert F. Rockwell, February 26, 1993, that he located the plaster in an antique shop near Newcastle, Maine, in 1983).

91. Central High School, *Manual of Administration,* third ed. (Tulsa, 1931), 15.

92. See Agreements between Dallin and Pietro Caproni, Treasurer, P. P. Caproni, March 15, 1913, and undated, 1913, AAA 178. Over the years Dallin signed various contracts with Caproni.

93. For a discussion of the *Appeal* in its possible early version and also other supplicant figures by Dallin, see Francis, 43-50 and 210-11, notes 28-46. See also Loring Holmes Dodd, *Golden Moments in American Sculpture* (Cambridge, Massachusetts, 1967), 37, and Greenthal, *Figurative Sculpture,* 276-[277].

94. See *Exhibition at St. Botolph Club, Boston. Paintings and Sculpture,* April 20-May 2, 1914, nos. 27 and 42.

95. C[harles] E. S. Wood, "Chief Joseph, The Nez-Percé," *The Century Magazine,* XXVIII (May 1884), 141: in this account, Wood wrote that Chief Joseph's words were delivered by "Captain John" before Joseph delivered himself up. For Wood's remarks years later, see Chester Anders Fee, *Chief Joseph. The Biography of a Great Indian* (New York, 1936), xi-xiii and 319-36. Norman B. Wood, *Lives of Famous Indian Chiefs* (Aurora, Illinois, 1906), 525-26, wrote: "During the Louisiana Purchase Exposition...Chief Joseph was one of the greatest attractions at the Indian Congress, the early part of the season. But the thought of exhibiting himself for money was very distasteful and humiliating to the proud chieftain.... He went back to the reservation the early part of July, but it was simply going home to die...." Alvin M. Josephy, Jr., ed., *The American Heritage Book of Indians* (n.p., 1961), 316, quotes Charles Wood: "...Standing back, he [Joseph] folded his blanket again across his chest...somewhat in the manner of a Roman senator with his toga...." Mark Stevens, "Chief Joseph's Revenge," *The New Yorker* (August 8, 1994), 29, compares Chief Joseph's remarks to Miles to the Gettysburg Address. Also see Binderbook: Gorham, Brown University, and Caproni Casts (1915), 6. Broder, *Bronzes,* 94-5, wrote, "...He [Dallin] made his first sculpture of an Indian in 1884, which he entitled *Indian Chief,*" and she identified The New-York Historical Society's bronze as a 1907 cast of the subject.

96. Roman Bronze Archives, Amon Carter Museum, 267, does not list the bronze.

97. "Beautiful Trophy for the Chicago Archery Meeting," and *The Jewelers' Circular*, LV (September 11, 1907), cover, AAA 182. Also see Christie's, *Important American Paintings, Drawings and Sculpture,* New York, December 3, 1993, no. 79. "Cyrus E. Dallin Tells James W. Reardon," *Boston Sunday Advertiser* [June 7, 1931], AAA 184: "...I learned it [archery] early as a boy, and shot as an Indian did...." Dallin was a champion archer, and once served as president of the National Archery Association.

98. Downes, 9.

99. *Caproni Casts* (1915), 7.

100. "Robbins Gift of Town Hall to Arlington Dedicated with Brilliant Ceremonies," *The Boston Herald,* June 26, 1913. Dallin wished to see Arlington renamed Menotomy, in recognition of the Native American settlement that had occupied the site. Dallin's two sculptures represent a collaboration with the architect R. Clipston Sturgis.

101. Clipping [Christian Science Monitor, May 11, 1912], and "Arlington Adds to Its Civic Group," both AAA 182.

102. Roman Bronze Archives, Amon Carter Museum: November 25, 1912, there is an entry, "Kneeling Ind. Hunter, S/105 [check mark]…145," but no other reference to *Indian Hunter* on page 267. The Arlington statue was cast by Roman Bronze.

103. *St. Botolph Club* (1914), no. 41; Trask, ed. *Catalogue De Luxe,* vol. 2, 434; clipping, [Kansas City Times, December 3, 1915], KCPL, includes *Indian Hunter* among the work he sold in San Francisco. A work titled *Indian Hunter Drinking* was exhibited in 1923 at Grand Central Galleries: High Museum of Art files.

104. Memorandum of Agreement between Dallin and the Massasoit Memorial Association, Incorporated, March 2, 1921, AAA 178; Charlotte S. Price, Curator of Books and Manuscripts, Pilgrim Society, to Mrs. Erwin Hutchings, June 17, 1976.

105. The first version of *Massasoit* (1914) was cast by Reed and Barton, and the second by Gorham. I wish to thank Nanepashemet, Director, Wampanoag Indian Program, Plimoth Plantation, who in his letter of January 14, 1993, pointed out the inaccuracies in the accessories of both versions of *Massasoit.* I also wish to thank Russell H. Gardner, Wampanoag Tribal Historian, for his information concerning the oral tradition that Dallin relied on descendants for models in order to assure the accurate physiognomy of Massasoit. See Alvin G. Weeks, *Massasoit of the Wampanoags* (privately printed, 1919), x-xi, and Frederick W. Bittinger, *The Story of the Pilgrim Tercentenary Celebration at Plymouth in the Year 1921* (Plymouth, 1923), 116-20. "Plan Statue to Massasoit," AAA 182, indicates, "A diligent search was made for the most accurate description of Massasoit.…" Also see note 62. Francis, 55-6, writes that Dallin used his friend John Singer Sargent's black model for *Massasoit*. One pastor in Winthrop drew an unfavorable comparison between the religious virtues of *Massasoit* and the pagan *Appeal to the Great Spirit*: "Bases Sermon on 2 Statues," AAA 182.

106. Roman Bronze Archives, 267, Amon Carter Museum, does not list the statue; "Marksmen to Flock to Boston in August," AAA 184; Sotheby's, *American Paintings, Drawings and Sculpture*, New York, May 27, 1993, no. 243.

107. Sotheby Parke Bernet Inc., *Important 19th and 20th Century American Paintings and Bronzes from the Collection of the Late Geraldine Rockefeller Dodge*, New York, October 31, 1975, and Patricia Janis Broder, "The Geraldine Rockefeller Dodge Collection of American Western Bronzes," *American Art Review*, III (March-April 1976), 109-21.

108. See Francis, 55-6 and 58-9. In the Dodge sale at Sotheby's (1975), the larger bronze, no. 120, was titled *The Passing of the Buffalo*, and the smaller, no. 75, *The Last Arrow*. Geraldine R. Dodge wrote to Mrs. A. M. Barron, Springville, May 10, 1941, about the large statue, "Mr. Dallin told me that sometimes it was called The Last Arrow or the Prayer for the Return of the Buffalo. I think the first title suits it best.…" In a typed manuscript (quoted by Broder and Francis), Dallin addressed the slaughter of the buffalo, and concluded, "My statue depicts the Indian standing with one foot resting upon a Buffalo skull, his last arrow gone…looking into the future with questioning soul.…" Both copies courtesy Frances Petty Sargent. Dallin criticized Buffalo Bill for slaughtering the buffalo: "Dallin Inspired by the Redskin," [Worcester Telegram], AAA 179.

109. National Sculpture Society: *Exhibition of American Sculpture. Catalogue*, April 14-August 1, 1923, 42, and *Exhibition of American Sculpture. Guide*, revised ed., May 3, 1923, 3. Alain Joyaux, Director, Ball State University Museum of Art, September 12, 1994, to Ahrens: "…As cast, the fist is solid versus open or drilled to actually hold a separate arrow. There are, however, sockets where the upper and lower sections of a two-part arrow would have been fixed…."

110. Grand Central Galleries, *Recent Sculpture by Cyrus E. Dallin, M.A., A.N.A.*, November 29-December 10, [1927], no. 17.

111. "Cyrus Dallin Dreams Great Memorial…," *Boston Sunday Advertiser*, November 22, 1925, AAA 184.

112. During the period c. 1880 to 1900 Dallin had executed a variety of academic subjects, most of which are known today only from photographs. For many years the photographer Stillman Powers recorded Dallin's work: "Mr. Dallin and I first met a little over 50 years ago when I entered the Massachusetts School of Art…. At that time he…was chief instructor in modeling and sculpture…. He made me his official photographer and he was a frequent visitor at my Studio and I at his. It was his custom to have me photograph his plasteline models sometimes in many views. He used the photos to study and also to send away for suggestions of placements…. Many of his fine creations were neither cast or placed because of the Depression and the World war…." Stillman Powers to Mrs. G. L. Barron, March 10, 1948, Scrap Book, SMA. Also see the typed ms., "Cyrus Edwin Dallin…A Biographical Sketch by Stillman Powers, 1950," AAA 179.

113. Francis, 112-14.

114. Files, Special Collections Department, University of Virginia Library. Information about Trowbridge's life courtesy Deborah J. Ervin, Local History Librarian, Robbins Library; the Library maintains a file related to the author along with a selection of his publications.

115. Cornelius Vermeule, *Numismatic Art in America* (Cambridge, Massachusetts, 1971), 160-62; also Greenthal, *Figurative Art*, 280-[81].

116. Mrs. Cyrus E. Dallin's Sterling Note Book, "Events in the Life of the Family…," AAA 178, and Vermeule, 162.

117. Francis, 131.

118. See AAA 178 for the 1930 agreement between Dallin and the Northeastern Section of the American Chemical Society for the Richards medal. Also see *Minute on the Life and Services of Theodore William Richards, 1868-1928,* AAA 181.

119. "Monument Dedicated in Woodbrook Cemetery at Woburn…," *The Boston Herald* [May 30, 1904], and an unidentified clipping, AAA 183. The two panels were cast by Henry-Bonnard. In a speech, "Heroes in Bronze," Dallin criticized Saint-Gaudens's allegorical figure on the Shaw Memorial, but he employed an allegory in Syracuse.

120. "The Long Story of the Hanover Battle Monument," *Hanover Herald*, September 30, 1905. The statue was cast by Bureau Brothers, Philadelphia. Material related to *The Picket* is found in the collections of the Hanover Area Historical Society.

121. Calvin M. Hennig, "The Outdoor Public Commemorative Monuments of Syracuse, New York:

1885-1950," doctoral dissertation, Syracuse University, 1983, 228, writes that there was a desire to erect a monument as early as November 1863. See *Extracts from the Proceedings of the Soldiers' and Sailors' Monument Commission of Onondaga County*, not paged. Additional information is found in the collections of the Onondaga Historical Association.

122. *Incident* was cast by Jaboeuf & Rouard, and *Call to Arms* by Gruet. Dallin's naturalism invites comparison with Saint-Gaudens's statue of *Admiral David Farragut* (1879-80) and Frank Simmon's *Navy Group* on the Civil War Memorial (1891), Portland, Maine. Sanborn (1909) mentions Dallin's experiments in Paris with a new method of enlarging from the small model to the large monument.

123. Wayne Craven, *The Sculptures at Gettysburg* (n.p., 1982), 24-30.

124. Mrs. Dallin's Sterling Note Book; also "The Sculptors Who Follow the Flag," and "An Inspiration to Nation's Defenders," AAA 180.

125. "Identifies Soldier Model," [July 2, 1918], AAA 181.

126. Clippings, AAA 181. Also F. Pfister, Jr., Gorham Corporation, to G. Bruce Braithwaite, Director, Springville High School Art Gallery, December 8, 1967: "We have...a bronze WWI Doughboy Statuette entitled 'Captured but not Conquered'.... This figure is of bronze and was made by Gorham in 1918...." Gorham records, Brown University.

127. Merriam Downes, "Captured But Not Conquered," AAA 181. For Halyburton as a prisoner, see "Sculptor Dallin Reveals Story of Famed Statuette's Creation," AAA 184.

128. "Sculptor Dallin Interprets Spirit of America's Returning Soldier Boy," AAA 182. See Agreement with Caproni, June 19, 1919, AAA 178.

129. "Impressive Scene at Sherborn Dedication," *Framingham Evening News*, October 14, 1924. Also see, "Sherborn Dedicates War Shaft Monday," AAA 182, and *Town of Sherborn, Massachusetts, 250th Anniversary* (Natick, 1925), 39-40.

130. The Agreement between Dallin and Mary Beecher Longyear, October 7, 1927, reads in part: "...The Sculptor shall...provide all materials and perform all work for said memorial in marble termed 'Spirit of Life' and will devote his best skill and energy to the making of said memorial as shown by the sketch model.... [He shall complete] Sketch model, on or before the seventh of October, 1927, clay figure on or before the first of January, 1928, completed memorial on or before the thirtieth of May, 1928.... The Sculptor may copyright the completed work, and...all preliminary studies and all models shall be the property of the Sculptor; but it is understood and agreed that the Sculptor shall make no plastic reproductions or reductions of the work without the written consent of the Owner...." Also see undated General Conditions for the Platform and Marble Superstructure, Gay and Proctor, Architects. Both AAA 178.

131. Agreement between Gorham and Dallin to cast *Spirit of Life*, February 23, 1928, AAA 178.

132. Dallin to Mrs. John M. Longyear, May 21, 1928, Longyear Museum and Historical Society.

133. L[eila] M[echlin], "The Spirit of Life," *The American Magazine of Art*, XX (November 1929), 603: "...Between two great works of art no comparison can be made. In this case each is distinctly individual. Mr. French has interpreted the spirit of life as upholding the life-giving water; Mr. Dallin has read into the allegory the continuance of life through rebirth—through succeeding generations. He has been most fortunate in representing a figure both vital and extremely still, a figure which partakes, as in great measure does Saint-Gaudens' Adams Memorial, of universal peace...." For information about the lives of Mr. and Mrs. John Munro Longyear, see Longyear Foundation, *Quarterly News*: 6 (Spring 1969); 8 (Autumn 1971 and Winter 1971-72); 11 (Autumn 1974). Information about the classical tradition is courtesy of David B. Whitehouse, Director, The Corning Museum of Glass. In a discussion of Dallin's ideal subjects, mention should be made of his *Alma Mater* (1916: Mary Institute and Saint Louis Country Day School, Saint Louis, Missouri), which is among his finest achievements: see W. K. Bixby Papers, Missouri Historical Society. Mary Institute had been established in 1859 under a charter granted to Washington University by Missouri to assure young women of Saint Louis an education equal to men. In 1915 William K. Bixby, a trustee of the estate of Mrs. William McMillan, and Edmund H. Sears, head of the school, sought to fulfill her wishes by creating a memorial to Mr. Sears. Since Sears felt a little uncomfortable about negotiating a monument to himself, a symbolic subject, *Alma Mater*, was finally selected. Instead of a competition to find an artist, Dallin was given the commission, with James P. Jamison responsible for the architecture. The specifications read in part: "The memorial shall consist of a group of three figures 'Alma Mater' seated and two young girls (as per sketch model).... Group to rest on a marble platform of pink Tennessee marble, and background with portrait bas-relief of Mr. Edmund H. Sears and inscription cut in same marble...." (Specification of Memorial for Mary Institute, and Agreement between Dallin and William K. Bixby, November 5, 1915). In selecting the subject, Bixby and Sears probably had in mind Daniel Chester French's *Alma Mater* (1903), but Dallin may have also seen the latter's *Gallaudet and His First Deaf-Mute Pupil* (1888).

134. Information courtesy Thomas C. Proctor, Assistant Director and Curator, Longyear Museum and Historical Society.

135. Longyear Foundation, "The Artist Speaks," *Quarterly News*, 3 (Spring 1966), not paged. The writer also commented: "When Mrs. Longyear saw the finished clay model...for the first time, she wrote in her diary in June 1922, 'It stood before us majestic, poised, conscious of the Truth of the Message she brought to the world.'..."

136. Ada M. Barron to Mrs. Cyrus Dallin, August 23, 1948, Scrap Book, SMA.

137. Minutes of the Mothers' Study Club, April 24, 1925, and Dallin to Mrs. [Anna] Johnson, March 17, 1927, Scrap Book, SMA.

138. Typed ms., undated, signed by Marguerete S. Sinclair, Secretary, Utah State Historical Society, Scrap Book, SMA.

139. "How Statue Is Made in the Marble," [Boston Post, February 15, 1915: Dallin's lecture at Museum of Fine Arts], AAA 180: "The human model first poses and a clay model about six or seven inches high is made. The next model is about two feet high and is called the working model. The next one is still of clay and is of the proportions desired for the statue proper.... When the big clay model is made...a plaster

paris cast is made of it and then, from this mould, a plaster reproduction…is obtained. From this the marble statue is next made, but the work of the sculptor is practically at an end.…" See also "New Dallin Statue Will Show the Indian Scout," [Christian Science Monitor, March 17, 1914], AAA 182.

140. Francis, 137-44.

141. Massachusetts Normal Art School, *Catalogue for the Twenty-Sixth Year, 1899-1900* (Boston, 1899), lists Dallin's teaching, "Modelling from Antique and Life; Composition," and *Massachusetts School of Art, 1937-1939* (n.p., n.d.), lists his faculty responsibility as, "Modeling from Life; Composition in Relief and the Round."

142. *Circular of the Massachusetts Normal Art School at Boston, Under the Direction of the State Board of Education. First Year, 1873-74* (Boston, 1873), [3]. Also see Paul Dobbs, "Massachusetts College of Art," *New England Archivist Newsletter*, 17 (October 1990), 21-2.

143. Undated handwritten testimonial, AAA 179. "Spirit of Life," Dallin's ms.: teaching did not bring Dallin a sense of economic security, which he felt always eluded him. A clipping, "The Fine Arts," AAA 182, mentions Dallin's modest art collection—including work by Barye, Frémiet, Cuyp, de Neuville and Corot. For reminiscences of Dallin as a teacher, see Ruth Christie Wheaton, July 8, 1989, and Ed Malsberg, June 16, 1989, to George Morgan, Massachusetts College of Art. Robert Alsen, Painted Post, New York, recalls playing as a boy in Dallin's studio while *Paul Revere* was being modeled; the artist was fond of children. On the other hand, certain anecdotes in Dallin literature reveal him to have been a somewhat feisty gentleman who relished a head-on encounter. Massachusetts College of Art recently acquired a plaster of Dallin's equestrian *George Washington*.

144. "Dallin, Utah Sculptor Visits His Old Home," [Deseret Evening News], AAA 180; "Mr. Dallin's Criticism," [Kansas City Star], AAA 182; "Sculpture as a Civic Asset," typed ms. fragment, AAA 179.

145. "Grant Statue Award. Controversy Deplored by Sculptor Dallin," AAA 181.

146. "American Sculpture. Its Present Aspects and Tendencies," *Boston Evening Transcript*, December 20, 1902; see also February 23, 1927.

147. Sanborn (1909).

148. "Cyrus Dallin, Famous Sculptor of Indian, Finds Appreciation of Art Waning in U. S.," AAA 179. He went on in this article to remark: "'Women in sculpture are so few because the woman is not as childlike as the man. Man is a boy. Women have sophistication; they have gone through experiences of which man has no conception.'"

149. "Sculptor Dallin on Art. His Lecture Last Night Before the University Club," [Salt Lake Tribune], AAA 180.

150. "Truth is Held Education Goal," *The Boston Herald*, December 13, 1936.

151. Seaton-Schmidt, 112.

CATALOGUE

Cyrus E. Dallin is the sculptor of work listed in the catalogue. Dimensions are in inches; in the case of rectangular objects, height precedes width. All inscriptions are oriented according to the *proper left* and *proper right* of the objects, not the viewer. Illustration numbers for objects correspond to catalogue numbers.

No. 1. *Algerian Panther*
1880
Terra-cotta, painted brown
Height: 8 3/4
Side of base at left: *ALGERIAN PANTHER / BY BARYE / COPIED BY DALLIN 1880*
Museum of Fine Arts, Boston. From the Estate of Isabella M. Hirst in her memory. 1980.403.

No. 2. *Lafayette*
1889
Bronze
Height: 42 3/8
Top of base at right: *C. E. Dallin / 188[?]*; top of base at left: *THIEBAUT FRERES / FONDEURS / PARIS*
National Museum of American Art, Smithsonian Institution. Gift of University of Pennsylvania School of Dental Medicine, Thomas W. Evans Collection.

No. 3. *President George Q. Cannon*
1891
Plaster
Height: 24
Back of bust: *C. E. Dallin / 1891*
Courtesy Museum of Church History and Art, Salt Lake City, Utah.

No. 4. *Angel Moroni*
c. 1891
Plaster, gilded
Height: 31
Courtesy Museum of Church History and Art, Salt Lake City, Utah.

No. 5. *Indian Head*
c. 1890s
Bronze
Height: 4 1/4
Front below neck: *C. E. Dallin* [illegible]; back: *The Henry-Bonnard Bronze Co. / Founders, N.Y.*
American Academy of Arts and Letters. Gift of Hamlin Garland, 1923.

No. 6. *Signal of Peace*
1890; cast c. 1923
Bronze
Height: 48 1/2
Top of base at left: © *C. E. Dallin / 1890*; side of base at right: *GORHAM CO FOUNDERS / QBMJ #3*

Collection of the Heckscher Museum, Huntington, New York. August Heckscher Collection.

No. 7. *Medicine Man*
1899
Bronze
Height: 16 3/4
Top of base at left: © *C E Dallin 1899*; side of base at right: *E. GRUET / JEUNE / FONDEUR / 44* [illegible] *AVENUE DE CHATILLON / PARIS*
Town of Arlington, Massachusetts.

No. 8. *Protest*
1904
Bronze
Height: 20 1/8
Top of base at left: *C. E. Dallin*; side of base at right: *ROMAN BRONZE WORKS N-Y-*
Springville Museum of Art, Springville, Utah. Gift from Hal and Aileen Clyde of Springville.

No. 9. *Appeal to the Great Spirit*
1913; cast 1921
Bronze
Height: 8 3/4
Top of base at left: © *C. E. Dallin 1913*; side of base at left: *#113*; side of base at rear: *GORHAM CO. FOUNDERS x* [scratched in] *QXC*
Collection of Sandra Rockwell Herron.

No. 10. *Appeal to the Great Spirit*
1913; cast c. 1919
Bronze
Height: 20 1/8
Top of base at left: *C. E. Dallin 1913*; side of base at right: *GORHAM Co Founders #37 /* [Gorham Trademark] *QPN*
Diplomatic Reception Rooms, Department of State. Gift of Philip L. Poe.

No. 11. *Appeal to the Great Spirit*
Modeled 1912; cast c. 1922
Bronze
Height: 39 3/4
Top of base at left: © *C. E. Dallin 1912*; side of base at right: *QAPU #7 / GORHAM Co. Founders*
Hood Museum of Art, Dartmouth College, Hanover, New Hampshire. Gift of Leslie P. Snow.

No. 12. *Appeal to the Great Spirit*
1912
Plaster
Height: 40 1/2
Top of base at left: © *C. E. Dallin 1912*
Rockwell Museum, Corning, New York. Gift of J. N. Bartfield Galleries, in memory of Jack N. Bartfield, on the occasion of Bob and Hertha Rockwell's fiftieth wedding anniversary and Bob's eightieth birthday, with additional contributions from the Board of Trustees, Rockwell Museum, and other friends.

No. 13. *The Scout*
Modeled c. 1912; cast c. 1916-24
Bronze
Height: 33 7/8
Right front corner at top of base: *C. E. D. / 1910*; side of base at right: *COPYRIGHT 1912 C E Dallin*; side of base at left: *GORHAM CO. FOUNDERS*; side of base at right: [illegible oval seal]
Ball State University Museum of Art, Muncie, Indiana. Gift of Frank C. Ball. 000.273.

No. 14. *The Scout*
1910; cast c. 1926
Bronze
Height: 22 1/2
Top of base at right: © *C. E. D. / 1910*; side of base at rear: *26 / GORHAM COMPANY FOUNDERS / Q 488*
Gilcrease Museum, Tulsa, Oklahoma.

No. 15. *On the Warpath*
1914
Bronze
Height: 42
Top of base at left: *C. E. DALLIN 1914* ©; side of base at right: *GORHAM Co. FOUNDERS*; side of base at left: *CAST ESPECIALLY FOR / THE PANAMA-PACIFIC INTERNATIONAL EXPO / GORHAM Co. FOUNDERS* [attached label]
Courtesy Mongerson-Wunderlich Galleries, Chicago, Illinois.

No. 16. *Indian Squaw and Child on Horseback* (title varies)
1920; cast c. 1924
Bronze
Height: 17 1/2
Top of base at right: © *C. E. Dallin '20*; side of base at rear: *GORHAM CO. FOUNDERS / QBZD*
Town of Arlington, Massachusetts.

No. 17. *War or Peace*
1905
Bronze
Height: 33 1/2
Top of base at right: *C. E. Dallin*; side of base at rear: *Roman Bronze Works / N.Y. 1905*
Springville Museum of Art, Springville, Utah. Gift from A. Merlin and Alice Steed Trust.

No. 18. *Standing Figure of a Native American Chief (Chief Joseph)*
1911; cast c. 1916
Bronze
Height: 25 1/2
Top of base at left: *Dallin 1911*; side of base at rear: *GORHAM CO FOUNDERS* [Gorham Trademark] *QAK Z 1*; top of base at front: *TO THEIR BELOVED SECRETARY / W. JOHNSON QUINN / FROM THE / TAVERN CLUB / THURSDAY JUNE 25, 1931*; top of base at rear: [illegible] / *BOSTON MASS*
The New-York Historical Society. Gift of Mrs. W. Johnson Quinn.

No. 19. *Archery Lesson*
1907
Bronze
Height: 18
Top of base at right: *C. E. Dallin / 07*
Collection of Michael D. Greenbaum.

No. 20. *Indian Drinking*
1912
Bronze
Height: 18
Top of base at left: *C. E. Dallin 1912*; side of base at right: *ROMAN BRONZE WORKS N-Y-*
High Museum of Art, Atlanta, Georgia. Gift of a friend of the Museum. 27.25.

No. 21. *The Marksman*
1912
Bronze
Height: 37
Top of base at right: *C. E. Dallin 1912*; side of base at right: *ROMAN BRONZE WORKS N-Y-*
Collection of Richard L. Fisher.

No. 22. *Indian Archer*
1915
Plaster
Height: 34 3/8 [figure]
Top of base: © *C. E. Dallin 1915*; underside of base, an aluminum tag with inscription: *P P Caproni Br. / Boston*
Giust Gallery (formerly P. P. Caproni and Brother), 1920 Washington Street, Boston, Massachusetts.

No. 23. *The Last Arrow*
1926
Bronze on marble base
Height: 15
Top of base at right: *Dallin 1926* ©; side of base at rear: [*PB & CO.*] *MUNCHEN Made in Germany*
Amon Carter Museum, Fort Worth, Texas. Purchase, Ruth Carter Stevenson Acquisitions Endowment.

No. 24. *Eastern Archery Association*
1920
Bronze medal
Diameter: 7 3/4
Obverse: *EASTERN ARCHERY ASSOCIATION*
Courtesy Ruth Dallin Stevenson.

No. 25. *Merion Cricket Club Medal*
Bronze medal
Diameter: 2 3/4
Obverse: *MERION / CRICKET / CLUB / MEDAL / NATIONAL / ARCHERY / ASSOCIATION / OF THE / UNITED STATES*; lower left quadrant: *C. E. Dallin*
Springville Museum of Art, Springville, Utah. Gift from Mrs. C. C. Trittin, Sandy, Utah.

No. 26. *National Archery Association*
1941; cast c. 1946
Silver medal
2 5/8 x 1 3/4
Obverse: below left foot: *C E Dallin '41*; *NATIONAL ARCHERY ASSOCIATION / OLYMPIC BOWMAN LEAGUE*; reverse: *1946 / VERNE TRITTIN / 803.6 / STERLING BALFOUR*
Springville Museum of Art, Springville, Utah. Gift from Mrs. C. C. Trittin, Sandy, Utah.

No. 27. *John Townsend Trowbridge*
1906
Plaster relief
15 7/8 x 11 15/16
Lower left: [*C E Dallin*]
Town of Arlington, Massachusetts.

No. 28. *John Townsend Trowbridge*
1906
Bronze relief
15 1/2 x 11 1/2
Lower left: *C. E. Dallin '06*; lower right: *T. F. McGANN & SONS CO / BOSTON MASS*
Clifton Waller Barrett Library, Special Collections Department, University of Virginia Library, Charlottesville, Virginia.

No. 29. *Pilgrim Half-Dollar*
1920
Silver coin
Diameter: 1 3/16
Obverse: between *HALF* and *DOLLAR*: *D*; upper left quadrant: *IN GOD / WE TRUST*; near rim: ⋆ *UNITED·STATES·OF·AMERICA* ⋆ *PILGRIM·HALF·DOLLAR*; reverse: near rim: ⋆ *PILGRIM·TERCENTENARY·CELEBRATION* ⋆ *1620-1920*
Anonymous Loan.

No. 30. *Two Models for the "Pilgrim Tercentenary" Half-Dollar*
1920
Plaster molds
Diameter: 13 3/4
Obverse: between *HALF* and *DOLLAR*: *C E D*; upper right quadrant: *IN GOD / WE TRUST*; near rim: ⋆ *UNITED·STATES·OF·AMERICA* ⋆ *PILGRIM·HALF·DOLLAR*; partially revealed title on book: *HOLY / BIB*; reverse near rim: ⋆*PILGRIM·TERCENTENARY·CELEBRATION*⋆ *1620-1920* (All inscriptions are mirror images.)
Museum of Fine Arts, Boston. Gift of a Friend of the Museum. 1981.66a, b.

No. 31. *Homage from Massachusetts to the Victorious Commander*
1921
Bronze medal
Diameter: 2 3/4
Obverse: lower right quadrant: *C E D*; along rim: *HOMAGE FROM MASSACHUSETTS TO THE VICTORIOUS COMMANDER*; reverse: *IN GRATEFUL / SALUTATION / FOCH / NOV. 14 1921*; lower left quadrant: *C E Dallin*
Springville Museum of Art, Springville, Utah. Gift from Gorham Silver Corporation, Providence, Rhode Island.

No. 32. *The National Arts Club, New York*
Bronze medal
4 3/16 x 3
Obverse: *THE·NATIONAL·ARTS·CLUB·NEW·YORK / FOUNDED 1899*; lower left: *V. D. Brenner 04*; lower center underside of ground line: *GORHAM*
Courtesy Ruth Dallin Stevenson.

No. 33. *Medal of Honor, Massachusetts Normal Art School*
c. 1924
Bronze medal
Diameter: 2 3/4
Obverse: lower right quadrant: *Dallin*; across face of medal: *MEDAL / OF / HONOR / M·N·A·S*
Springville Museum of Art, Springville, Utah. Gift from Mrs. Bertram Dallin.

No. 34. *Beverly Hospital Incorporated*
1930
Bronze medal
Diameter: 2 3/16
Obverse: lower left quadrant: *Dallin / 1930*; along rim: *·BEVERLY HOSPITAL·INCORPORATED 1893*
Springville Museum of Art, Springville, Utah. Gift from Gorham Silver Corporation, Providence, Rhode Island.

No. 35. *Theodore William Richards Medal*
1930
Bronze medal
Diameter: 2
Obverse: below arm of bust: *Dallin*; along rim: *THEODORE WILLIAM RICHARDS MEDAL 1868-1928*; reverse: *AWARDED FOR / CONSPICUOUS / ACHIEVEMENT / IN / CHEMISTRY / BY / THE NORTHEASTERN / SECTION OF THE / AMERICAN CHEMICAL / SOCIETY INC. / TO*
Springville Museum of Art, Springville, Utah. Gift from Glenn Doherty, Newberry, Massachusetts.

No. 36. *Captured But Not Conquered*
1918
Plaster
Height: 33 1/8
Top of base at rear: © *C. E. Dallin / 1918*; front of base: *CAPTURED / BUT NOT / CONQUERED*
Town of Arlington, Massachusetts.

No. 37. *Captured But Not Conquered*
1918; cast 1918-19
Bronze
Height: 32 1/2
Top of base at rear: © *C. E. Dallin / 1918*; front of base: *CAPTURED / BUT NOT / CONQUERED*; side of base at rear: [illegible]
Springville Museum of Art, Springville, Utah.
Gift from Gorham Silver Corporation, Providence, Rhode Island.

No. 38. *Mine Eyes Have Seen the Glory*
1919
Plaster
Height: 36
Top of base at right: © / *C. E. Dallin 1919*; front of base: *MINE EYES HAVE SEEN THE GLORY*
Town of Arlington, Massachusetts.

No. 39. *Sketch for War Memorial, Dedham*
Pencil on paper
7 1/2 x 7 1/2
Below figure in drawing: *INSCRIPTION*; across bottom: *Sketch for war memorial Dedham / Cyrus E. Dallin*.; upper left: [illegible stamp]
Town of Arlington, Massachusetts.

No. 40. *Model of a World War I Memorial for Arlington*
Plaster and wood, painted
19 5/8 x 21 11/16 x 11 3/4
Front: *THE WORLD WAR / IN MEMORY OF THE SONS / OF ARLINGTON WHO GAVE / THEIR LIVES AND SERVICE / IN THE WAR FOR HUMANITY*; back: *THE WORLD WAR* [eight names that seem to be imaginary]
Town of Arlington, Massachusetts.

No. 41. *Mr. and Mrs. John Munro Longyear*
1927
Plaster relief
18 1/8 x 17 7/8
Longyear Museum and Historical Society, Brookline, Massachusetts.

No. 42. *Mary Baker Eddy*
1922
Clay
Height: 19 5/8
Longyear Museum and Historical Society, Brookline, Massachusetts.

No. 43. *Self-Portrait Bust*
1927
Bronze
Height: 16 3/4
Front, below bust: *DALLIN*; back of neck, along edge: *T. F. McGann & Sons Co / Boston Mass*
Springville Museum of Art, Springville, Utah.
Gift of Mothers' Study Club of Springville.

No. 44. *Emmeline B. Wells*
1928
Plaster
Height: 27
Below bust: *EMMELINE B. WELLS*
Springville Museum of Art, Springville, Utah. Gift from Kolob Stake Relief Society, Springville.

No. 45. *Appeal to the Great Spirit*
Metal pattern
Height: 22 1/2
Top of base at left: © *C. E. Dallin 1913*
Courtesy Textron Inc.

No. 46. *Paul Revere*
Modeled 1899; cast late 1970s
Bronze
Height: 35 1/2
Top of base at right: *C. E. Dallin '99*; side of base at right: *COPYRIGHT BY C. E. DALLIN, Sc. PAUL REVERE / MFA* ©; side of base at left: *WASATCH BRONZEWORKS, LEHI, UTAH*; *MFA* (in two overlapping squares surrounded by a circle)
Museum of Fine Arts, Boston.

Not illustrated: see Fig. 7.

Design: Marilyn Jones

Printing: Princeton Polychrome Press

Archival Paper